THE
SCAM
HANDBOOK

THE
SCAM
HANDBOOK
THE SECRETS OF
THE CON ARTIST

JOEL LEVY

BARNES & NOBLE BOOKS
NEW YORK

This edition published by Barnes & Noble, Inc.,
by arrangement with Elwin Street Limited

2004 Barnes & Noble Books

Copyright © Elwin Street Limited, 2004

M 10 9 8 7 6 5 4 3 2 1

ISBN 0-7607-5345-8

Conceived and produced by
Elwin Street Limited
79 St. John Street
London EC1M 4NR
www.elwinstreet.com

Editor: Debbie Foy
Designer: Simon Osborne
Illustrations: Richard Burgess

Printed in Singapore

Picture Credits
The publisher would like to thank the following
for permission to reproduce images. While very
effort has been made to ensure this listing is
correct and to contact the copyright holders of
the images, the publisher apologizes for any
omissions and would welcome contact from the
copyright holders for correction in subsequent
editions.
Associated Press: 27, 38, 121, 126, 133
Corbis: 16, 40, 63, 110, 140
Getty Images: 113, 123
Kansas Historical Society: 104
Photolibrary.com: 29, 57
Photonica: 33, 95, 143
The Picture Desk: 7, 10, 13, 14, 21, 23, 35,
45, 53

CONTENTS

INTRODUCTION

Chances are that at some point in your life you've been taken for a ride – hustled, grifted, bilked, conned, or scammed. You may not be sure how it happened, but you're damn sure it won't happen again. There is no surer way to protect yourself against the wiles and ways of the confidence artist than to learn about them from the inside, and that's what this book can help you achieve. You'll learn all the secrets of a successful con artist and successful conning, from the psychological attributes that make the con artist tick, to the ins and outs of scams ancient and modern.

Ever since the Snake first talked Eve into tasting the apple, the con artist has been practicing his art; the art of confidence. Confidence is the key, because once you gain people's confidence you can manipulate them. In con artists' parlance, that person becomes a mark – also known as a sucker, dupe, john, jake, green, rube, apple, bates, or Mr Goodman – ready to be played in a confidence game, big or small. In Genesis, the Snake was practicing what is known as a short con – a confidence game where the con artist only comes into contact with the mark once. A con game that requires the con artist and mark to come into contact more than once is known as a long con.

In the modern era, traditional distinctions like these are increasingly out of date, because most scams and cons take place without any actual contact with the mark whatsoever. E-mail, telemarketing, and even text-messaging are the media through which con artists mainly

The Original Con: The myth of Adam and Eve portrays the Snake as a sly, dishonest trickster who duped Eve into eating the forbidden fruit.

practice today, but many of the con games they employ are simply variations on themes established long ago. Laying bare both ends of the scamming spectrum, this book explains the workings of many classic scams and brings you up to date with the most prevalent of the new con games, including identity theft and credit card cloning.

ABOUT THIS BOOK

Divided into two sections – The Players and The Scams – the first section looks at each of the major elements of the confidence game, analyzing the mind and morality of the con artist and what makes him tick. The psychology of the mark is also explored, explaining what qualities and attributes make a person a good mark, where to find the biggest suckers, and why marks so rarely complain about being scammed. The various types of accomplice who may accompany con artists in their work are outlined here, too. This section also delves into the anatomy of the confidence trick itself, explaining the technical terminology you'll need to know to understand cons and scams on their own terms and it looks at the forces arrayed against the con artist, including the law enforcement and private agencies that try to prevent and punish fraud and scams.

Section two looks at the scams themselves, taking you step-by-step through each one, explaining how they are set up, how the mark is drawn in, how the con artist moves in for the kill, and how he makes off with the loot. This section explores the all-time classic scams, including the basic street cons that all fledgling con artists start off with, to some of the most familiar cons in modern culture – gambling cons, white collar scams, cons that target heart, health, hope, and spirituality, plus frauds for the Information Age. "Con Culture" box features explore the role of the con artist in society and literature and mini reviews dotted throughout the book entitled "Scams on Screen" look at how cons and con artists have made an impact on the cinema, providing a guide to the best in scam films.

Scattered throughout the text is the con artist's Hall of Fame – a cavalcade of extraordinary characters who have garnered infamy, fortune, and (usually) a sticky end. Within the Hall of Fame are tales of murderous greed, overwhelming ambition, fatal delusion, and corporate corruption, reaching from the séance rooms of Victorian England to the boardrooms of Enron. Though incredible yarns in their own right, these stories graphically illustrate the perils, pitfalls, and finer points of the con artist's trade.

To help you unravel the language of the con artist and his world, a glossary explains all the unusual or con-specific terms used in the book.

MORAL HEALTH WARNING

If a "How To" guide for immoral or criminal activities seems ethically suspect, bear in mind this moral health warning. Although the following chapters outline the key elements of successful con games and accomplished con artists, they also make clear that among these are: a total disregard for other human beings; an absence of healthy psychological attributes such as a conscience, or empathy; and a willingness to live a lonely and hunted existence. In particular this book emphasizes that every would-be con artist is also a potential mark, and in doing this, shows you how to avoid fulfilling that potential. Knowing your enemy is the best way to avoid his traps. The truth is that this is a book for people who want to avoid being a mark, rather than for people who want to become con artists. Don't be a sucker!

THE PLAYERS

Section 1: page 10

THE CON ARTIST

Con artists consider themselves to be the princes (or princesses) of the criminal fraternity – a cut above the other crooks on the street. The successful con artist is suave, smooth, smart, accomplished, and sophisticated. He doesn't have to resort to violence like a heavy, flash a piece like a gangster, or break and enter like a common-or-garden burglar. In fact, the con artist hardly considers himself to be a crook at all.

CON ARTIST CHARACTERISTICS

Being a con man isn't for everyone. It is a special kind of person who can convince someone to place their trust in a perfect stranger and give them something for nothing. It is an even more unusual person who can take money from the old, the needy, and the foolish without a twinge of conscience or a moment's hesitation. To psychiatrists, this kind of person is known as a sociopath.

Psychopathology of the con artist
A successful con artist needs to be missing some psychological attributes that the rest of us take for granted.

Conscience
This is top of the list. There's no room for recriminations when fleecing an elderly citizen out of his life's savings, or ripping off a sick person desperate for a cure.

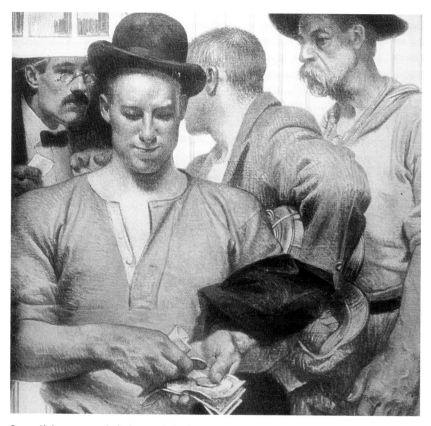

Con artists are experts in human behavior and since time began people have been duped, swindled, tricked, or conned into handing over money for fraudulent deals.

Responsibility

A con man absolves himself of any responsibility for crimes committed. The con artist's mantra is "they had it coming." In other words it serves the suckers right if they get taken. Many con artists actually convince themselves that it's the sucker's fault he got ripped off – if he hadn't been so greedy, stupid, or trusting he'd still be in possession of his dough.

Health quackery scams, such as the marketing of "miracle cures" to restore hair, prolong youth, aid weight loss, and cure cancer, traditionally target the ageing and vulnerable.

Respect

The con artist believes that the world is divided into suckers and those who are clever enough to take advantage of them. People in the former category don't deserve to hang on to their money. The way the con artist thinks, this is the natural order of things; the way of the world. And this is how he rationalizes away any twinges of conscience he may feel about fleecing vulnerable marks.

Faith

The con artist has no faith in human nature. He believes that everyone else in the world is as amoral as him, it's just that they pretend to have morals and he doesn't. So, he rationalizes, he's more honest than everyone else! Given, therefore, that it's a dog-eat-dog world, the con artist's second mantra is "do it to them before they do it you."

Bonds

A successful con artist has no interest in forming meaningful relationships, friendships, or partnerships. First of all, being tied down will likely compromise his work and put him in danger of getting caught. Secondly, the con artist doesn't trust anyone, which tends to make many relationships difficult.

WATCHING THE DETECTIVES

CONNING AS LAW ENFORCEMENT

Sometimes it's the detectives who do the conning, often employing the popular "con-by-letter" scam, along the lines of: "You've won a prize – just send us your credit card details or a small advance fee to claim it." Police around the world have used this type of ruse to get wanted criminals and other law-breakers to come to them. Bogus prize certificates are sent out to a group of criminals or law-breakers inviting them to the competition runner's head office. The certificates are printed with an ID number, but unbeknown to the criminal, it's actually the number of his arrest warrant or FBI ID Order. When the criminal turns up at the convincingly decked out offices and hands over the prize certificate he is promptly arrested.

Hard work is for suckers

The con artist's third mantra is "hard work is for fools." Why should he sweat and slave like some ordinary Joe when he could be living it up on easy street? Why punch in and out, pay taxes and kowtow to the system, when you could be your own boss, raking in the cash and living the high life? Ironically a good con artist displays many of the virtues he affects to despise because a successful con requires hard work as well as grift.

Cash is for the taking for a successful con man. To his way of thinking, the virtues of hard work, honesty, and integrity are for suckers who don't know a better way.

What a rush

Finally, the best con artists genuinely love what they do, getting a thrill out of pulling a successful con. Proving that you are smarter, sharper and faster than the other guy provides quite a rush. Pulling a scam is like playing a game – winning that game affirms the con artist's self-image as someone who is a cut above the rest of the pack.

THE SUPPORTING CAST

Some scams can be pulled by one guy working alone. In many ways this is the best option, because the more people who are involved the more complex the scam becomes and the more scope there is for disaster. Also, bringing in help means trusting someone, which can also be a big mistake for a con artist.

Short con associates

However, to work the scam successfully and get the really big pay-off a con man may need support from one or a variety of associates. How the supporting cast is described depends on whether the con being pulled is a short or a long con. When carrying out a short con the cast list reads something like this:

The Con Man

This is the main guy who masterminds and, if necessary, bankrolls the operation.

The Advance Man

He checks out the locale and stakes out potential marks. He also scouts around for getaway routes and possible sources of trouble.

CON CULTURE

THE CON IN SOCIETY

The con artist occupies a cherished place in modern culture, but his roots can be traced far back in time and analyzed on three levels:

The changing man

The con artist is a figure of charm and dangerous fascination. He breaks all taboos without conscience, living out forbidden desires and inhabiting any role he chooses, as he pleases. Secretly, there is a part of everyone that yearns for an unfettered conscience and a changeable existence.

The lovable rogue

The con artist represents the acceptable face of the underworld. Tales of cons and con artists comfort society by offering the myth of the lovable rogue and his "honor among thieves." The con artist helps to alleviate the discomfort society feels when contemplating the violent, evil criminal.

Tricking the Devil

The most deep-seated appeal of the con artist comes from his association with the trickster, which features in the folklore of almost every recorded society. The trickster can take any form. To American Indians he took the form of a coyote or spider; in European folklore he appeared as Jack the Giant Slayer; and in the modern era he even appears as Bugs Bunny or Daffy Duck. Here, the trickster is a con artist using a ruse to gain the confidence of his suckers and duping them for gain or amusement. The con artist and his games remain popular as they enable us to feel we can assert our individuality in a restrictive and overbearing society.

The Roper

He attracts the mark's attention and "ropes" him or her into the con. Also known as the catch or the steerer.

The Shill

This guy poses as an ordinary member of the public – someone just like the mark – but who is really a plant. For instance, the shill can increase the mark's motivation to take part by "winning" some money from the con artist to show the mark that it can be done.

The Muscle/Heavy

A good con doesn't involve any violence, but sometimes it's a good idea to have back-up just in case the mark gets fractious. Often just the threat of violence is enough to "block hustle" the mark (i.e. prevent him from doing anything to recover his money).

Long con associates

In a long con, the cast list might include the short con characters but may also feature two other roles:

The Middleman

A sort of glorified roper, the middleman's job is to get the mark interested and involved, taking him through introductory steps that don't involve committing any real money, before meeting . . .

The Inside Man

The guy supposedly in charge, who the mark believes he has to impress to get his pay-off. Usually the inside man is the con artist himself, though it could be another accomplice acting as a front.

HALL OF FAME

Pope Joan: The papal impostress

Name: Joan/Johannes Anglicus
Nationality: English
Years as a con: Unknown
Amount earned: Unknown
Years in jail: 0

The story of Pope Joan, the only female pope in the long history of the papacy, is generally regarded as a fable, but for around four hundred years it was regarded as truth, and many today still argue for its veracity.

Posing as someone you're not is a common practice in cons of all types, but it is unlikely that anyone ever pulled off an impersonation to match that of Joan, AKA Johannes Anglicus, AKA John of Mainz. Since this story is today generally regarded as a fable, the biographical details of Joan's life are sketchy, at best. In fact, no one even knows if she was called Joan. The earliest versions of the story talk about a priest called Johannes (i.e. John) – it was only natural to change the John to Joan when the cross-dressing ruse was discovered. Even her nationality is uncertain. Some sources say Johannes Anglicus (i.e. English John), but others say John of Mainz. A recent popular novel based on the story styles the papal impostress as Joan of Ingelheim. Supposedly, Joan studied as a man in Athens, a center of learning in ninth-century Europe, and showed an extraordinary aptitude for education. She quickly became a top scholar and went to Rome, the destination of choice for any ambitious young person, to lecture at the Trivium. Going under the identity of an English clergyman named John, she attracted the attention of learned men thanks to her unequaled knowledge of science, and she became a popular and respected figure. John was elected Cardinal and, on the death of Pope Leo IV, was elected Pope John VIII. Joan ruled as pope for two years during which her secret was known only to one attendant. Somewhat foolishly, given the risks she had overcome to get this far, she then became pregnant by this unhelpful accomplice. Joan concealed her growing bump, but disaster struck while she was out riding, as on a public street the baby decided to enter the world. Her secret uncovered, Joan quickly fell victim to rough Roman justice. After suffering the pain and humiliation of giving birth in public, she was then tied by the ankles behind her horse and dragged through the streets while being pelted with stones.

The curia adopted a sex check as part of the papal coronation ritual. The pope sits on a marble chair with a hole in it (known as a "bath stool") supposedly so that his genitals can be examined. To this day, papal processions avoid the narrow street where Joan supposedly gave birth.

Is there any truth to this incredible story? The Catholic Church insists that it is merely a legend, pointing to the absence of contemporary records. The street is avoided by papal processions, they argue, because it is narrow, while the bath stool became part of the papal installation ritual simply because newly elected popes would sit on it to take a break during their inauguration wanderings. Pope Joan enthusiasts insist, however, that the story is true and that the Church is simply covering up its embarrassment at having been so spectacularly scammed.

THE MARK

A good con man knows that almost everyone is a potential mark. There are plenty of people out there who think they're too smart to ever fall for a scam. These people make excellent marks. On the other hand, there are plenty of gullible fools out there – they also make good marks. Practically any personality trait or weakness of character can make someone vulnerable to scamming.

TYPES OF MARK

Although absolutely anyone can be a mark, there are some types of people who get scammed more consistently than others.

The elderly

According to some estimates, up to 60 percent of marks are people over the age of 65. Whether or not this is true, there's no doubt that the elderly make vulnerable and easy targets with several features that make them attractive to con men. They are often reasonably well off, with considerable savings. They are likely to be trusting of people who seem authoritative – for example, cops, doctors, accountants, etc. They may be a little slower or more easily confused than others. They are often both lonely and chatty, and it's therefore easy to strike up a conversation and find out sensitive or profitable information. They are often at home or out and about but in no great hurry, again making them easier to target. Finally, con artists know that the elderly often don't report fraud for fear of being thought senile.

Ill people

The sick or infirm may not always be thinking clearly, and may be desperate for any slim hope of relief or a cure.

Small business owners

Big businesses are more likely to have anti-fraud procedures and personnel, so con artists prefer to target small business owners who may be worth a substantial amount of money but have fewer precautions to prevent fraud.

Believers

Fake psychics and healers are among the most common types of con men (see Chapter 6). They depend on willing believers – for example, suckers who want to believe in such things as astrology, psychic searching, fortune telling, contact with the dead, faith-healing, or magic cure-alls. Such people are characterized by their lack of critical thinking and selective attention to evidence, making them easy prey.

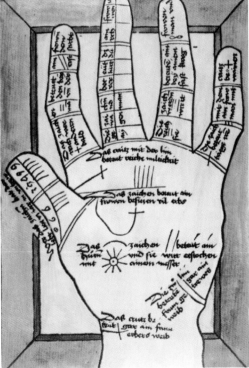

Con artists don't merely seek out the greedy and weak, they also seek out the needy.

Horses for courses

The infinite variety of marks does not mean that the same scam, or even the same scammer, will work on everybody. Quite the opposite. The good con man knows that succeeding with a scam means picking the right mark and playing the right role for that mark. This is why rich people are as vulnerable as poor people and the young as vulnerable as the old. They might be alert and suspicious of characters who don't conform to their preconceptions of trustworthiness, but this makes them more likely to fall for the character who does. For instance, a rich person is automatically suspicious of a bum but more accepting of the opposite – someone who seems wealthy and cultured.

THE PSYCHOLOGY OF THE MARK

The mark is motivated by two basic drives. They may seem opposed and even mutually exclusive but quite often they work in tandem.

Greed

Everyone wants to get something for nothing. Some people want it so much they're willing to forget that it's impossible. The mark's greed is what makes scams from the pigeon drop to the pyramid scheme possible. But some marks are not so much greedy as *needy*. Perhaps someone has a unfulfilled desire that they would like to play out, say, for example, to become a pop star. A successful con artists will tap into this desire.

The desire to trust

It is often said that these days people are much more cynical, but the vast majority would still rather believe that a person is genuine. Faith in human nature runs deep. The con man's job is to take advantage of this.

Using psychology
Other psychological phenomena the con man can use include:

The halo effect
People who are attractive, smartly dressed, articulate, and self-assured are automatically invested with other qualities for which they have exhibited no evidence. These qualities include intelligence, trustworthiness, and competence; all useful in a con artist's repertoire of tricks.

The conformity urge
It is difficult to go against the wishes, attitudes, and judgements of the majority. If everyone else is saying or doing something, there is a natural urge to go along with them. This is where shills or accomplices can come in handy since they appear as ordinary citizens who are prepared to go along with the "performance" the con man is giving. The poor old mark gets hooked in because he can see others doing so and he doesn't want to miss out on a good thing.

The authority effect
Most cultures train people to respect authority figures, meaning that the mark is less likely to question the motives of a con man playing the role of an authority figure, or even simply talking in an authoritative fashion.

The "Barnum Effect"
This describes the tendency to believe that positive attributions apply to you – for example, if the con man says to the mark, "I can tell that you've made some pretty shrewd moves with your investments although you're not always given credit for it." Compliments like these flatter the mark's ego and make him eager to prove the con artist right.

Frank Abagnale Jr: Swinging through the 60s

Frank Abagnale Jr AKA Frank Williams, Robert Conrad, Frank Adams, and Robert Monjo, was a prodigy in the world of con artists who had amassed a multi-million-dollar fortune, posed successfully as an airline pilot, and slept with countless women throughout the world, all before the age of 21.

Between 1964 and 1969, Abagnale passed $2.5 million in fraudulent checks in every state in America and 26 foreign countries besides. A high-school drop-out with an IQ of 136, he successfully impersonated a doctor, an attorney (fabricating a Harvard law degree, but genuinely passing the Louisiana Bar Exam), a sociology professor at Brigham Young University, a stock broker, and even posed as an FBI agent. His notorious escapades as a pilot for Pan Am earned him the dubious title "The Skywayman." Abagnale started his life of crime as a runaway kid aged just 16 (although being tall and prematurely gray he looked much older). Perhaps his first act of forgery was to change one of the numbers on his driver's license to make him seem 10 years older. He used fake ID to cash small checks at hotels around New York, until one day he spotted a flight crew leaving a hotel. Attracted by their air of self-confidence and glamor, he decided on a new direction and quickly rounded up everything he needed to become a fake Pan Am airline pilot.

He posed as a pilot whose uniform had been stolen to get a "replacement" uniform; he posed as a small airline owner to get a printing firm to make him up a pilot's ID as a "sample"; and he got a mail order certificate company to send him a framed pilot's license using fake information, which he then had reprinted in wallet-size to use as a

Name: Frank Abagnale Jr
Nationality: American
Years as a con: 5
Amount earned: $2.5M
Years in jail: 5

form of identification card. Thus equipped he was able to get free flights around the country with other airlines who also paid for his food and hotel bills and charged it all to Pan Am. Being an airline pilot lent him credibility, enabling him to cash fake pay checks which he used to entertain and impress women wherever he went.

Impersonation wasn't the only scam Abagnale pulled. One of his early scams was to change the numbers on generic bank deposit slips to his own account number, using magnetic ink. Every time someone paid in a check using one of these, the slip was scanned and the money diverted to his account. By the time the bank got wise to the scam he had collected $40,000 and had changed his name.

Today, Abagnale deeply regrets both his life of crime and the more sensational aspects of his book, and although he says that he's honored that Steven Spielberg, Leonardo Di Caprio, and Tom Hanks participated in a movie that was inspired by his life, he is at great pains to point out that it is partly fictional.

STAKING THE MARK

Good groundwork is essential to a successful con. First it's essential to gain as much knowledge as possible about the mark, whether practicing a short con on a passerby or a long con on a meticulously researched target.

Instant feedback

The more skillful the con artist, the more he can "read" the mark simply through observing and talking to him or her. In this sense, a good con man is like a detective, carefully observing every clue the mark presents. What type of clothes is he wearing? What sort of car is she driving? Is he thin or fat, old or young? Does she seem expensively attired or just trying hard to look wealthy? Making such judgements does have its dangers, however, because they depend on assumptions and generalizations. To get more specific information the con man simply talks to the mark.

Cold reading

Extensive research by psychologists has uncovered the techniques used by con men and women, such as psychics and mind readers, to get information from someone without their knowledge. The process is called cold reading and all con artists use it when necessary. Though most scammers are not trained in the art of cold reading, they have simply picked it up as a consequence of their natural abilities. The core tactics of cold reading include:

Proceed from the vague to the specific

Start off with general statements and use the mark's verbal and non-verbal feedback to figure out which ones are accurate. Then use these to make more specific guesses.

Claim the mark's input as your own

If the mark gives you information, simply talk as if you knew that already.

Use the "Barnum Effect"

See page 25 for a full explanation of the psychology of the Barnum Effect. It rarely fails to get the mark on your side.

Deeper research

For long cons, or simply to get his bank details, it's often necessary to know more about the mark. The more knowledge about personal details the con man can demonstrate while in conversation with the mark, the more likely the mark is to assume that everything is legit. Useful ways to find out personal details include:

Gold is the con's best friend. Many people have been defrauded out of their life savings with "lost" gold mine scams. If it sounds too good to be true, it usually is.

Info in the public realm

Use the phone book, the public records office, the Internet (for example, by "Googling" the mark – typing his name into the search engine, Google, to see what comes up), or, for rich and/or famous marks, use magazines such as *Forbes* in the US or *Tatler* in the UK. A good deal of information can be gleaned from these sources if the cunning con artist knows where to look.

CON CULTURE

THE CON IN LITERATURE

The con artist features in the earliest literature and the oral traditions that preceded it. Odysseus is one of the first con men whose exploits were actually written down (for instance, sneaking into Troy or slipping past the Cyclops with cunning ruses).

But it was in America that the con artist in his modern guise was to prove most iconic. In his book on Oscar Hartzell (see page 116), *Drake's Fortune: The Fabulous True Story of the World's Greatest Confidence Artist*, Richard Rayner explains: "There are no folk heroes more 'all-American' than con artists. Though we may openly condemn them, deep down we admire their bravado; their shrewd understanding of how to rouse ambition and greed in their hapless victims. They offer the American dream on the quick, and, after all, don't suckers get what they deserve?"

From Herman Melville's *The Confidence-Man: His Masquerade* to the hard-boiled pulp of Jim Thompson (author of *The Grifters*), the con artist has served as what Gary Lindberg, author of *The Confidence Man in American Literature*, calls a "covert cultural hero."

Cold calling
Most marks will assume that anyone calling them who is already in possession of their name, phone number, and address must be legitimate.

Phishing
An increasingly popular method of scam research, this involves sending an official-looking e-mail asking for personal/banking details or redirecting a mark to a website which does the same.

Trash
Going through trash to find old bills, statements, or letters may seem like dirty work but this practice can uncover pure gold for the con man.

WHY THE MARK NEVER SINGS

One of the primary reasons that con artists con is that they hardly ever get caught. Partly this is due to the way that law enforcement deals with fraud and scams (see Chapter 3), but largely it is because the mark almost never tells anyone. Just one in seven, or, according to some estimates, as few as one in 10 marks files a complaint with the police. There are four main reasons for this:

Resignation
Many marks are well aware that cons are a low priority for law enforcement, especially if less than a few thousand dollars have been scammed. They also realize that without real names, addresses, or records of any kind, it will be virtually impossible to prove anything to anyone. They feel it is better just to write it off to experience and continue on their way, sadder but wiser.

Embarrassment/shame

The mark may not realize that anyone can fall for a scam and that millions regularly do. In fact he may feel like he's a loser and the only idiot who could have fallen for a con like this, so the last thing he wants to do is admit to anyone that he's been taken. As we saw earlier, some may have particular reasons for not wanting to 'fess up – for example, the elderly may be anxious that their relatives will think them incapable.

WATCHING THE DETECTIVES

PERSONAL SERVICES

In the course of finding true love, lonely and vulnerable women (and some men) often discover they have been the victim of a particularly callous con. Private investigation agencies are now offering background-check services for potential partners as a routine measure before accepting a date. For instance, the Women's Fraud Recovery Center is a PI agency that specializes in running background checks on men to help women avoid falling victim to the cruelties of what has become known as the "Sweetheart Scam" (see page 96). For $59 they will put together a comprehensive dossier detailing the man's current and previous address information dating back nearly 20 years; references from relatives and neighbors; criminal history, including conviction and jail history; vehicle registration history; civil judgement and child support order history; bankruptcy and real estate history; and any evidence of the use of multiple identities or social security numbers. The same agency also offers help in tracking down con artists who have made off with a woman's loot, and even with finding out what assets they might have.

Fear

Many scams have built-in block hustles or tricks to stop the mark reporting the scam. If the scam seemed illegal in nature, the mark may be worried about getting in trouble with the law. If it involved the underworld in some way, the mark may be worried about future retribution from gangsters. A prop sometimes used by con men is the cackle-bladder – a squib of fake blood that can be used to make it look like someone got shot. An action guaranteed to send the mark scurrying for cover, never to emerge.

Cognitive dissonance

Sometimes the mark doesn't sing because he simply refuses to believe that he's just been swindled. When the mark's beliefs about himself (for example, that he is shrewd and capable guy who, perhaps, holds down a good job and keeps a family of four) conflict with the evidence (that he just got played for a complete fool by a cunning con artist), he experiences what psychologists call cognitive dissonance. This feeling is psychologically very disturbing and must be resolved either by changing his beliefs, which may be difficult, or his perception of the evidence. In other words, it's easier to believe that you didn't really get swindled and that the scheme will pay off eventually, than it is to believe that you're not so clever after all and you've been had.

Being conned can be devastating, so many marks don't admit it, even to themselves.

THE HEAT

Getting caught may be rare for the con artist, but cons and scams are still illegal, and very expensive for the businesses that have to cough up to cover losses. This means that, ranged against the con artist, are the twin forces of public law enforcement and private enterprise – an army of cops, agents, investigators, private eyes, lawyers, and other anti-fraud specialists.

SCAMS AND CONS IN LAW

Terms like "scam" or "con," although descriptive, have no real legal definition. According to the penal codes of most countries, the crime involved when a con artist performs a scam on a person or company is called fraud, and this comes in many varieties. The two main types of fraud are:

Actual fraud
This is where the con artist conspires intentionally to cheat the mark – for instance, by telling him or her that by paying X amount up front they will get Y in return, when in fact the mark will get nothing.

Constructive fraud
This is where the con artist misleads the mark through words or actions – for instance, by promising that Preparation X will make the mark more attractive to women, when in fact Preparation X is sugar-water. Other crimes that a con artist might get charged with include wire fraud – a con

or scam perpetrated over the telephone or Internet; fraudulent use of the mails – a con or scam that involves the postal service (for example, because the pitch is made by letter); or a variety of financial fraud categories that cover investment and banking frauds. Scam-related categories of crime include forgery and impersonation (for example, of a police officer – see the Bank Examiner Scam, page 68).

THE LAW

For those few marks who do summon up the courage or wherewithal to report a swindle or scam, the proper avenue of complaint differs depending on the exact nature of the scam. In most Western countries there are several levels of jurisdiction as far as fraud is concerned – local, national, international, and specialist (for example, financial or Internet).

Call the cops!
For pretty much anything except a high-value fraud, the mark needs to approach the local police department. The definition of "high-value"

Scams such as X-ray vision, in which quacks claim to be able to "see" diseases in the body, are difficult to police as susceptible marks are desperate to believe in them.

WATCHING THE DETECTIVES

PSYCHIC DETECTIVES

When the police or other law enforcement agencies have run out of leads they sometimes call in so-called psychics for a little bit of help "from the other side." It's unclear just how common this supernatural sleuthing is. According to the American TV channel CBS, one survey shows that 35 percent of urban police departments have used psychics at one time or another, but police forces don't like to admit to using psychic detectives. "Cops by nature are skeptical. They don't like to talk about this stuff, and it doesn't make it into the reports most of the time for obvious reasons," says one New Jersey police chief.

The official line is rather different – in the US, for instance, despite claims by numerous "psychic detectives" that grief-stricken relatives will often look to the spiritual world when conventional policing has turned up few leads, the FBI and the National Center for Missing & Exploited Children both insist that psychic detectives have never helped to solve a case.

The skeptics have put the detective skills of some psychics to the test. In controlled trials they proved to be slightly worse than "ordinary" members of the public at psychically "reading" crime-related material for clues about the crime. But detailed analysis of the way they work shows that "psychic detectives" use a number of tricks to make themselves seem more accurate than they really are, including making more guesses than an average punter (and therefore, presumably, having more chance of being right), giving very extended, detailed descriptions that cover a lot of bases, and making vague predictions that are open to multiple interpretations. It seems likely that the real skills of "psychic detectives" lie in the arena of self-promotion.

obviously varies, but in the UK, for instance, dedicated fraud squads are not interested in losses less than £750,000 (roughly $1.15 million)! In America many police departments have "bunco squads" (from a traditional term for a scam), with officers who deal with cons such as Three-Card Monte, Pigeon Drops, short changing, and ATM scams.

Serious fraud squads

The next level of fraud investigation operates at a more or less national level, and gets called in when fraud involves a lot of money or has other serious features. In America and Australia, for instance, a fraud case that crosses state boundaries might call for the involvement of federal authorities (the FBI or the Australian Federal Police). The feds might also get involved if the fraud centered round the mail, the banks, or the stock market, although in these cases specialist departments might be more appropriate.

In Britain, the biggest police forces may have their own fraud squads, while the Serious Fraud Office deals with major, complex frauds. In America, the FBI and the Secret Service both tackle fraud on a national level and fraud with international links. In Australia, the National Fraud Desk of the Australian Bureau of Criminal Intelligence deals with complex fraud with an international "flavor." At international level, police forces liaise through organizations such as Interpol, which do not deal with members of the public directly, but exist purely to provide support services and information pooling for the cops.

The specialists

In response to the increasing incidence of Internet fraud and identity theft new agencies have been set up – for instance, America has the Internet Fraud Complaint Center and the Federal Trade Commission.

Sante and Kenny Kimes: Mommy and Clyde

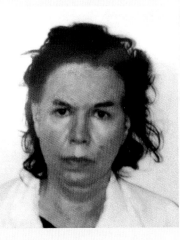

Name: Sante and Kenny Kimes
Nationality: American
Years as a con: 40 and around 10
Amount earned: Unknown
Years in jail: 120 and 125

The inspiration for the movie *The Grifters*, the story of Sante and Kenny Kimes, AKA "Mommy and Clyde" is a horrifying mix of cons and cold-blooded murder.

Sante Louise Singhrs was born in July, 1934 in Oklahoma, but her family soon moved to California where it broke up, leaving her to run wild as the daughter of a prostitute. She was eventually adopted and taken to live in Carson City, Nevada, where she became Sante Chambers. In all, she was to rack up some 28 different aliases during her career.

After two failed marriages and an arrest for shoplifting, Sante Singhrs slipped into a life of prostitution and crime. In 1965 she was arrested for auto theft after taking a car for a test drive and failing to return it. She ran up a considerable charge book all over Southern California. In 1971 she hooked up with a millionaire property developer Kenneth Kimes. Together, the two formed an unholy alliance. Attempting to gain publicity for a Bicentennial scam they forged a memo on White House stationery asking for an interview with President

Nixon's wife and later crashed a reception for Vice-President Gerald Ford. Sante was also continually being arrested for stealing and insurance fraud and then her slavery scam was revealed. For several years she had staffed her house with illegal immigrants, lured off the streets and kept under house arrest as slaves in the various Kimes's homes, where they were viciously abused. Her husband cut a deal with the feds, but Sante eventually wound up in jail (not before trying to skip custody by crawling through a hospital window) for three years.

Young Kenneth Kimes Jr was born in 1975 and grew up in an atmosphere of control, abuse, and criminality. When he went to college in the 1980s, his mother went with him and their union soon became unhealthily close. When Kenneth Sr died in 1994 she hid it from the world, probably because his will excluded her and possibly because they were not legally married. When various associates started to make trouble over this or her other fraudulent scams, they ended up dead, probably with the assistance of her son. Between 1990 and 1998, the Kimes family lawyer and two business associates were shot dead.

Then in 1998 the mother and son team embarked on their final fraud. They rented an apartment owned by an elderly New York socialite, Irena Silverman, and murdered her. They intended to use forged documents to claim that Silverman had sold them the property and then taken a long vacation. They successfully dumped the body but were betrayed to the FBI.

At their trial in 2000 they were found guilty of murder and given huge sentences. In a sensational postscript, Kenny tried to escape from jail by taking a TV reporter hostage with a ballpoint pen. Currently they face the death sentence in California.

Many victims of cons and frauds don't report them either because they don't know where to file a complaint, they are afraid of possible retribution, or they fear looking foolish.

Regulatory bodies such as the Securities and Exchange Commission police the financial world, while offices of fair trade and Better Business bureaux regulate businesses and competition and also oversee the rights of the consumer.

Faith in law enforcement

To the untutored eye the various agencies and bureaux seem to boast considerable manpower and large budgets, but the truth is that for the ordinary mark the law is ill-equipped to help. Fraud experts complain that fraud squads are too under-resourced, under-staffed, and ill-experienced to cope with the complexities of modern con games.

There is also often a widespread attitude among both the public and law enforcement agents that con games are essentially "victimless crimes" low on the list of crime-fighting priorities. Often the same justification beloved of the con artist will be reeled out: "Cons and scams aren't real crimes – no one gets hurt and nothing gets physically stolen." Combine these problems with the natural obstacles to investigating and successfully prosecuting con artists – lack of evidence (partly because the mark was originally colluding with the con artist), confusion over the legal aspects, difficulty in tracing cash and people with assumed identities, witnesses too embarrassed to speak out – and it starts to become obvious why the average mark won't get much joy from a complaint, and still less from an attempt to get his or her money back.

PRIVATE ENTERPRISE

The manifold failings of official law enforcement mean that many people and businesses turn to private fraud specialists for help with prevention and justice. In fact, internal fraud prevention and detection by companies is the most effective way of stopping or catching con artists. A survey in Australia showed that internal company controls provide the most common single method of detection, accounting for 48.1 percent of successful interventions. Companies are also increasingly turning to private "fraud busters" such as the Association of Certified Fraud Examiners (professionals similar to accountants).

Watchdogs

The individual mark can turn to either big consumer organizations or opt for more personal help. Consumer organizations offer advice, warn marks of potential dangers, and help to collect information on con artists that can then be forwarded to the authorities. In the US, for example, the National Consumers League has set up both the National Fraud Information Center and Internet Fraud Watch. There are also websites such as Fraud-Aid.com that act as an on-line fraud victim support service

SCAMS ON SCREEN

SÉANCE ON A WET AFTERNOON (1964)

Star rating: *****
Director: Bryan Forbes
Starring: Kim Stanley, Richard Attenborough
Cons: A Cassie Chadwick-style crooked psychic scam (see page 50) only with a kidnapping to replace the blackmail.

THE STING (1973)

Star rating ****
Director: George Roy Hill
Starring: Robert Redford, Paul Newman, Robert Shaw
Cons: Based around a Big Store con (see page 74) featuring a convincer, stall and button, complete with cackle-bladders.

and provide advice on how to spot a con, how to avoid being scammed, and what to do if you are. Some scam-prone professions, such as the direct marketing and telemarketing industries, set up their own bodies to help protect consumers and set codes of conduct. Most countries now have a direct marketing association and provide people with the chance to join a register to opt off mailing lists.

The best enforcement money can buy

On a more personal basis a mark can get help from private detectives or lawyers. Private investigation can track down a con artist and his assets when state law enforcement doesn't have the time, resources, or motivation, and a good lawyer can protect the mark's interests and set in train processes to recover any stolen assets. Just because law enforcement agencies won't always take action, doesn't mean that con artists are immune to the power of the law.

The fourth estate

The weapon that the con artist most fears is publicity, which makes the media the most powerful ally that a mark can have. Con artists depend on a veil of anonymity and secrecy to keep marks in the dark while they operate with impunity. As soon as their methods or faces become known, the well of marks will dry up and the hustler will find himself in hot water. An excellent example of this is shown in the career of Frank Abagnale Jr (see page 26), one of the most successful con artists of modern times. Abagnale's prolific hustles and scams were finally cut short when he became internationally recognizable. His initial arrest happened when an airline stewardess recognized him at a French airport, and when he subsequently escaped in New York he was quickly recognized on the street and picked up again.

ANATOMY OF A SCAM

At all points in human history the underworld has developed as a separate community from legitimate society, with its own rules and traditions and its own language. Within the underworld different professions have evolved their own specialized jargons, as impenetrable as the technobabble of the engineer or computer programmer, helping to exclude the uninvited mass of marks.

The world of the con artist is no exception. While almost all cons follow a roughly similar pattern of pitch, sting, and get away, the enormous variety of moves in the con artist's game has led to a marvelous but mystifying proliferation of descriptive and evocative language. This chapter provides a quick primer to that language, explaining step-by-step the anatomy of a scam in the con artist's own terms.

THE SET-UP

Some cons can be improvised on the spot (and a good con artist is a master of improvisation), but the biggest and most successful scams need preparation.

Areas of opportunity

The expert con artist knows his territory – the street layout, the joints with friendly or obliging management, the local law and whether or not they can be bribed (this is known as "having the ace" or "the fix"), and the local heavies and whether or not they need to be mollified.

Though times have changed for the con artist, the anatomy of a scam has remained the same and versions of eighteenth-century cons are still played out today.

He also knows the best spots to find marks, although actually working these spots is often left to accomplices whose job it is to rope or steer the mark into the con. Today, as in days gone by, the most fruitful hunting grounds are areas where travelers congregate and change from one mode of transport to another – train stations, bus depots and airports. Con artists who work these spots are known as "depot workers."

Places like these are full of people who may be tired and a little disoriented, and are frequently carrying money, credit cards, passports, and other valuables.

Trains, buses, boats, and ships have many of the same virtues, together with passengers who are fretful and bored, and ready to be interested in friendly conversation or potentially profitable diversions. The riverboat gamblers and railroad hustlers were the original aristocracy of American grifters, while the cream of European con artists worked the trans-Atlantic cruise liners, bilking the high rollers.

Today the most rapidly developing area of opportunity for the con artist is "virtual space" – an imaginary location from which the con artist operates via the Internet, telephone line, or cell phone. He can fool the mark into thinking he's anywhere, without ever having to leave home.

Taking the right angle

The good con artist knows which angle to take with which mark. To con a rube you need to play the honest Joe. To con a high roller you need to first gain his implicit approval by the way you dress, talk, and live. For any high-end-type con, involving a fake business deal, for instance, or trying to catch the eye of a rich widow, it's necessary to spend a little to get a lot. The con artist needs to be seen driving the best car, staying at the best establishment, and smoking the most expensive cigars. This is known as "putting on the dog."

The pitch

The pitch or build-up, where the con artist attempts to draw the mark into the con (usually by proposing something that seems to offer the mark a way to make money), is all-important. In a short con the pitch may be straightforward and short, but in a long con it may have several stages. For instance, most Big Store cons (a con based around a phoney establishment, such as a fake bookies or brokerage) involve a convincer – something that draws the mark further into the con, convincing him that it's legit. The most common convincer is allowing the mark to make or win some money (often paid out of his own initial investment). Alternatively there's the stall, where the mark is temporarily prevented from getting more involved in order to increase his motivation.

Closing the deal

At the end of the set-up stage comes the "send," where the mark is sent home or to the bank to get his money (in the nineteenth century this was often known as the "country send"); and the "hurrah," where the mark is drawn in to such an extent that he is fully committed to seeing the con through (for example, because he has invested all his savings in

SCAMS ON SCREEN

HOUSE OF GAMES (1987)

Star rating: *****
Director: David Mamet
Starring: Lindsay Crouse,
Joe Mantegna
Cons: The movie is built around a card game based Big Store con (see page 74), and features a hot seat and block hustle. Focuses on the lore of this infamous con.

DIRTY ROTTEN SCOUNDRELS (1988)

Star rating: ****
Director: Frank Oz
Starring: Michael Caine,
Steve Martin
Cons: Starts off with money-for-petrol-type hustles, but graduates on to Spanish Prisoner scams (see page 86), with Caine impersonating exiled minor royalty.

expectation of a big pay-out). If the mark is reluctant, suspicious, or anxious the con artist can prod him into action using a form of deadlining, where the mark is warned that the window of opportunity is closing and he needs to act fast to take advantage, or the threat of "red-inking," where the mark is threatened with being left out of the deal and missing out on the spoils.

THE STING

The "sting," where the con artist moves in for the kill and relieves the mark of his money, can also take several forms. In a bait-and-switch-style con, where the mark is scammed by being promised one thing and left with another, the all-important stage is the shift or the switch. This is where the con artist uses misdirection or sleight of hand to swap one thing for another (for example, an envelope full of money for an envelope

SCAMS ON SCREEN

THE GRIFTERS (1990)

Star rating: *****
Director: Stephen Frears
Starring: Angelica Houston, John Cusack, Annette Bening
Cons: Bening plays variations of the Badger Game (using sex to dupe the mark) and Cusack practices short con gambling hustles.

SIX DEGREES OF SEPARATION (1993)

Star rating: *****
Director: Fred Schepisi
Starring: Will Smith, Stockard Channing, Donald Sutherland
Cons: Smith passes himself off as the son of a famous actor in this typical "high-society impersonator" ruse.

full of strips of newspaper). In the "tear-up," the con artist appears to release the mark from his obligations so that he leaves without argument – typically this takes the form of pretending to tear up the mark's check, which has in fact been palmed and switched with a blank piece of paper.

THE BLOW-OFF

The "blow-off" is the end of the con, where the con artist gets rid of the mark and makes good his getaway. This may involve simply disappearing and moving on to another locale or decamping to enjoy the fruits of victory. Favorite getaway spots include the Bahamas, Switzerland, Florida (a popular jumping-off place to the Bahamas), Panama, Belize, and Antigua.

The block

However, the really well-worked con has a built-in "block hustle." This is where the mark is prevented from beefing (complaining about the swindle to either the con artist or the authorities) through one ruse or another (see Chapter 2).

EQUIPMENT

Since the essence of the con game is to use psychology to convince the mark to hand over his money himself, props are usually kept to a minimum. However, there are some important tools that feature in many cons. The "mich roll," short for Michigan roll, is a rolled wad of blank paper or small denomination bills wrapped in a few high-denomination bills, handy for convincing the mark that he's looking at a large amount of cash.

HALL OF FAME

Cassie Chadwick: Claim to fame

Cleveland's most famous con artist started life as simple Elizabeth Bigley, but by the end of her career she was the wealthiest and most sought-after high-society high roller in Cleveland.

Born in Eastwood, Ontario, in 1857, Bigley was the daughter of a humble working man and apparently decided that she needed a life of luxury without effort. Under various aliases, including Lydia Scott and Madame Lydia De Vere, Elizabeth started to fleece the people of San Francisco under the guise of a hypnotist, fortune teller, or healer.

In another ruse that dates back at least as far as Thackeray's *Vanity Fair*, she found that by playing the grand lady she could take advantage of the extensive credit that would be offered by willing shopkeepers, merchants, and bankers. Elizabeth/Lydia would sweep into town, take a suite in the most expensive hotel or hire a mansion, entertain on a lavish scale and spend, spend, spend. By 1893 she was living as "Mrs Hoover," resorting once more to the fortune-telling scam. She hired private detectives to research the backgrounds of her clients, amazing them with detailed knowledge of their personal lives and histories. This tactic is still widely used today, and is known as "hot reading" (as opposed to "cold reading" – see page 28).

In 1897 Mrs Hoover (known to her friends as Connie) married Dr Leroy Chadwick, and promptly hatched her greatest scheme yet. At a dinner party she met a prominent lawyer named James Dillon and learned that he was soon to visit New York. She subsequently arranged to "bump into" Dillon in New York and asked him to escort her on an errand. To Dillon's amazement they arrived at the house of one of

Name: Constance Cassandra Chadwick
Nationality: American
Years as a con: 25
Amount earned: $1M
Years in jail: 5

America's richest men and best-known philanthropists, Andrew Carnegie. Connie went inside and spent half an hour talking to servants, pretending to be inquiring after the references of a potential maid-servant, although Dillon did not know this. Returning to the carriage she "accidentally" let fall a piece of paper. Retrieving it, Dillon was astonished to see that it was a promissory note for $2 million, signed by Andrew Carnegie! It was, of course, a forgery. Swearing Dillon, a notorious gossip, to strictest confidence, Connie admitted that she was Carnegie's illegitimate child that he doted on her, and had given her around $7 million in securities.

Dillon duly spread Connie's story and banks fell over themselves to offer her unlimited credit. For seven years she lived the high life, borrowing at least $1 million (according to some sources as much as $20 million). Connie was finally exposed when a local businessman asked for repayment of a loan. The securities were revealed as forgeries, and in November 1904, Connie was unmasked. In March 1905, Connie Chadwick was convicted of conspiracy to fraud, fined $70,000, and sentenced to 14 years, although she died in custody in 1907.

Ringers

A "ringer" is something worthless that can be swapped for something of value (or that contains something of value) – for example, a bag of torn up newspapers that can be switched for a bag of money. Typical ringers include the "Spanish" handkerchief (see The Jamaican Switch, page 78) and the gold bar that was used in a successful nineteenth-century scam. This was a bar of lead painted gold, sometimes with a small plug of real gold in one end, which could be sampled by the mark and taken to an assayer.

Magic wallets

The magic (or lost-and-found) wallet is a prop that featured in a series of successful scams invented by William Elmer Mead in the early twentieth century. The magic wallet is an expensive-looking wallet stuffed with

SCAMS ON SCREEN

THE LAST SEDUCTION (1994)

Star rating: *****
Director: John Dahl
Starring: Linda Fiorentino,
Bill Pullman
Cons: Playing a highly successful female con artist, Fiorentino pulls a variety of impersonator scams and insurance frauds.

THE SPANISH PRISONER (1997)

Star rating: ***
Director: David Mamet
Starring: Campbell Scott,
Steve Martin
Cons: Does not actually feature a Spanish Prisoner con, but a blend of Jamaican Switch (page 72) and Bank Examiner cons (page 68).

money and also containing documents, papers, invoices, and cards which combine to suggest that the owner is wealthy, successful, and/or famous, thus setting up the mark who finds it. Similar devices (for example, a suitcase full of suggestive or highly sensitive documents) are still used in scams today.

The "magic wallet" features in a version of the Pigeon Drop scam in which the mark is asked for advice in return for a "share" of the money.

THE SCAMS

Section 2: page 54

The Classics

Today's con artist can choose from an array of media when it comes to perpetrating a scam, with the Internet and the telephone proving ever more popular (see Chapter 9). Many of the scams themselves, however, have stayed much the same or are simply new twists on old hustles that have been performed for hundreds of years. This chapter looks at some of the classic scams that form part of every con artist's book of tricks; hustles that the true con professional took in with his mother's milk, and which are second nature him. It is best to be clued up about these scams, because you never know where, when, or in what form you might encounter them.

The roots and origins of many of these classic scams can be traced back to the nineteenth century or even earlier. They have entered the modern con artist's lexicon via the world of the nineteenth-century American con artists and gamblers; people like the notorious Railroad Hustlers and the infamous Ben Marks (see pages 70 and 74 respectively), who formed a conning community that developed its own jargon, codes of conduct and folklore, and has since assumed a legendary place in the annals of confidence trick history.

But these New World scammers and hustlers were simply building on tricks that had been brought over from the Old World, cons and tricks that have probably been practiced in some form or another since the beginnings of civilization.

THREE-CARD MONTE

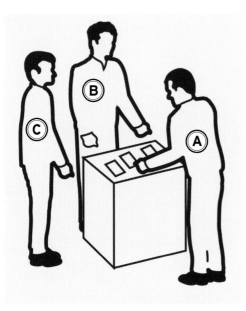

The Players
a. The Con Artist
b. The Accomplices
(the shill, muscle, look-out, roper)
c. The Mark

Also known as the Texas Twist or the Country Boy, Find the Lady in Britain and Bonneteau in France, the Three-Card Monte is the mother of all card cons. It's not just for small fry, either; in 1999 one highly gullible mark in Colorado, US, was taken for over $27,000. Remember: the hand is quicker than the eye. A good con artist cannot lose.

The Set-Up

1. Two or more people are standing around a cardboard box on a busy street. The dealer has three cards; two are black and one red. The red is usually a queen. The dealer shows all three cards, lays them face down on the table and rapidly picks up one card with his left hand and the other two with his right hand, and drops them back on the table in new positions. He repeats this scheme a number of times. The onlooker has to bet the position of the card which is alone in its suit (i.e. the queen).

2. Someone always seems to be winning; this person is the accomplice or shill, working alongside the dealer with the intention of luring unsuspecting marks.

3. Additional accomplices will include the look-out, who watches for the cops and signals their approach so that the game can be folded up quickly; the roper, who seeks out the marks; and the muscle man, who takes care of anyone who tries to complain.

The Sting

4. The mark is persuaded to join the game. He never wins.

5. The dealer holds two cards in his right hand. The upper card is held between thumb and forefinger and the lower card is held between thumb and middle finger, with a small gap between both cards. According to common sense, the dealer should drop the lower card first, but his forefinger surreptitiously ejects the upper card first, which causes the mark to lose track of the right card. This is especially difficult to see if the dealer's hand makes a sweeping move from his left side to his right side while he drops the cards.

6. If the mark does happen to bet on the right card, the dealer can employ various tactics. These will include accepting instead a wrong bet from a shill and refusing the mark's bet on the grounds that only one bet can be taken at a time, or swapping the cards while the mark's attention is distracted, or simply arranging for the table to be knocked over and declaring the deal void.

Variations

Amateur con artists will employ a muscle man to grab the mark's wallet and run, or pick the pockets of the mark as he is busy watching the game.

Christopher Rocancourt: Friends in high places

Name: Christopher Rocancourt
Nationality: French
Years as a con: around 16
Amount earned: $Millions
Years in jail: 4 to 5 (due out 2007)

Operating under a profusion of aliases, French-born con man Rocancourt, AKA Fabien Ortuno, James Fox, Christopher Reyes, Prince Galitzine Christo, Christopher De Laurentiis, Christopher de la Renta and, most recently, Christopher Rockefeller, lived the high life in Hollywood and the Hamptons while bilking millions from the gullible rich and hanging out with celebrities.

Rocancourt conforms to the classic con artist's profile writ large. Although he insists that he is not really a thief or a crook, and was simply borrowing money that he meant to repay, he has been involved in an array of swindles, frauds, and criminal activities from diamond smuggling and jewel theft to investment fraud and possession of hand grenades! He's skipped bail and broken the law in at least three countries, but has claimed to be friends with the actors Jean-Claude Van Damme and Mickey Rourke plus Bill Clinton and the Sultan of Brunei.

Rocancourt's story begins, like many con artists', with an unhappy childhood. Born in Honfleur, France, in 1967, to a drunk and a prostitute, he spent time in care and ended up on the streets of Paris. However, by the 1990s he was living in the expensive Regent Beverly Wilshire hotel in Beverly Hills, L.A., posing as, variously, the son of film producer Dino De Laurentiis and nephew of fashion designer Oscar de la Renta. When he checked out in 1997 he owed the hotel $60,000. In an interview with *60 Minutes*, conducted from a jail cell, he explained, "I like to pay hotel bills, but it's just very expensive, you know?"

Rocancourt funded his lavish lifestyle by scamming rich marks for millions, promising huge returns on investments or charging fees for arranging non-existent deals and loans. He was picked up in 1998 after a nightclub shoot-out but skipped bail, turning up in the Hamptons, New York State, posing as the European heir to the Rockefeller fortune. Claiming to be Christopher Rockefeller, he continued to scam money from wealthy marks and run up huge hotel bills. He was picked up again by police after local people became suspicious that the Rockefeller heir was driving a Mazda, and in 2001 police finally netted him.

In May 2003, after writing a book about his life while in prison, Rocancourt was extradited to New York to face charges of fraud and plea-bargained his way out of a 20-year sentence, landing just five years, less the time already served. His victims are currently seeking financial restitution, but as Rocancourt's attorney explains, "Whatever funds there were have been used up." Right up to the end, Rocancourt exhibited classic con-man psychology, arguing that his victims were to blame for falling for his tall tales, and that there is a world of difference between his antics and "real" crime. In a *New York Times* interview just months before his final arrest he said: "I would not consider myself a criminal. I steal with my mind."

THE PIGEON DROP

The Players
a. The Con Artist
(AKA the rope or catch)
b. The Accomplice
(the cap)
c. The Mark
(AKA the pigeon)

A classic con that is just as popular today as it ever was, this scam has many variations and subtle permutations. The essential element is the mark's unquestioning trust of authority.

The Set-Up
1. The con approaches a likely mark, usually a guy at a shopping mall or outside a bank. He or she engages him in conversation.
2. The con finds a package nearby. The package happens to be stuffed with dollar bills and a note that explains that the cash has been illegally obtained, possibly something to do with drugs.
3. The con asks for the mark's advice in return for a share of the money. Together the con and the mark work out what to do.

The Sting

4. The accomplice comes into the conversation, saying he has overheard and offers to help, in return for a split of the money. He has a "friend" – a lawyer or accountant – who lives nearby and who has some expertise.

5. The accomplice goes to speak to his "friend." The con continues to befriend the mark, turning on the charm. The accomplice returns. His "friend's" advice is that the money can be shared, after putting it away safely for a month or so.

6. The con and the accomplice suggest that the mark hold the money for a month until it can be cashed safely. The mark agrees.

7. The con persuades the mark that he should put up some "good faith" money to show that he won't be tempted to run off with the contents of the package. The mark is persuaded to hand over this money before the con hands over the package.

8. The amount of money the mark hands over will depend on the nature of the scam. It could be anything between $150 and $15,000, but it is usually around $5,000.

9. The con and the accomplice exchange addresses and telephone numbers with the mark and then depart.

10. The mark is left with the package. What is inside is a mich roll, comprising of a couple of dollar bills wrapped around a wad of paper. By then the con artist will be a long way away.

Variations

There are now many variations of this classic scam, including the con artist claiming to have a winning lottery ticket for thousands of dollars. "I am an illegal immigrant and therefore cannot collect the winnings," he will say. "I will give you half of the money if you cash the ticket in." Don't fall for this one.

CHANGE RAISING

The Players
a. The Con Artist
b. The Mark

One of the most basic classic scams in the book, change raising is eschewed by all except the common street hustler, but also provides a handy fallback scam for con artists down on their luck who need to make a quick buck. The change-raising scam is also strictly for the heartless and unfeeling, since the luckless cashier or store clerk who falls for it could end up being accused of having his or her fingers in the cash register.

The Set Up
1. The con artist walks into a corner store or up to a newsstand and buys a low-value item, such as a pack of gum or a candy bar – anything that costs just under a dollar. He pays for it with a $20 bill.
2. He receives in change one $10 bill, one $5 bill, four $1 bills and some loose change.
3. Feigning mild dismay at the mass of change (which is even easier if in a country that uses coins instead of bills for single units – for example,

pounds or euros), the con artist asks the clerk if he can change a five and five ones for a ten.

4. Crucially, he waits for the clerk to hand over the $10 bill before handing over his wad of bills, which actually consists of a five and four ones. When handing it over he tells the clerk he thinks that's right but that he'd better count it.

5. The clerk does so and points out that it's a dollar short.

The Sting

6. The con artist says something like, "Oh – sorry! Here you go – actually, no, you know what? I could do with a $20 bill. You've got nine there – if I give you a one and a $10 bill, can you give me twenty?"

7. The clerk, thoroughly confused by now but wanting to be helpful, hands over a $20 bill and the con artist leaves the shop $10 richer. The scam revolves around the fact that the $10 bill he gives the clerk in return for the twenty was actually the store's money, not the con artist's.

8. If the clerk gets wise, it's easy enough to apologize and explain that it was a genuine mistake. Or the con artist can be really brazen and challenge the clerk to try to explain exactly what was wrong with the exchange – which can be harder than it sounds.

Variations

So long as the key step – getting a bill as change and then using it to get a bigger bill as change – is adhered to, this scam can be done for any size of bill and using any excuse. For instance, the con artist could make it obvious that he's in a hurry while asking the clerk for $10 in return for the five and four ones, and then, on "discovering" that he's short a dollar, could become impatient and return the original item together with a dollar and $10 bill, and ask for his $20 back.

HALL OF FAME

Madame Therese Humbert: Leading society scammer

Name: Therese Humbert
Nationality: French
Years as a con: 20
Amount earned: $20M
Years in jail: 5

Responsible for one of the great scandals of turn-of-the-century Europe, Madame Therese Humbert used a fundamentally simple but devastatingly effective ruse to borrow an immense fortune and become one of the most powerful women in France.

Madame Humbert used a variation on the fake inheritance scam worked to such great effect by Cassie Chadwick (see page 50), but her version of it was even more outrageous. Humbert and her husband claimed to be the possessors of a vast inheritance from an American millionaire called Robert Henry Crawford. The inheritance, roughly $20 million in bearer bonds, was sealed in a box, kept inside a safe. The story put about to explain the inheritance depends on the source.

According to one source, Humbert claimed that her good fortune was just rewards for tending to a sick but wealthy businessman, Robert Henry Crawford, while traveling on a train in 1879. In other versions of the tale, Humbert was rumored to be Crawford's illegitimate daughter embroiled in a legal battle with his nephews for Crawford's inheritance.

Astonishingly, French banks and many wealthy individuals were happy to lend the Humberts millions of francs with no more security than this flimsy story. In addition, Humbert offered lenders impossibly generous terms, paying higher interest rates than anyone else in the market. Greed overcame any doubt, and the Humberts were soon swimming in money. Humbert's millions gave her access to and influence with all of the most important people in the country, and she became a leading society hostess, welcoming cabinet ministers, bankers and captains of industry to her salons and chateaux around the country. Some lent her money as a form of bribe to secure advancement, and it was said that she could make or break a man's career in *Belle Epoque* France.

Humbert's income depended on loans, which accrued interest, some of which sooner or later had to be paid. Soon she was sucked into a kind of high-stakes Ponzi scheme (see page 130), where she would acquire ever larger loans to pay off the old ones. Her downfall was inevitable, but incredibly she brought it on herself by taking umbrage at the extortionate rates of interest she was being charged and launching a suit accusing lenders of usury. People started asking the obvious questions and soon calculated that there could not be enough money in the mythical box to pay off all the debts.

Finally, in 1902, the box was opened to reveal . . . less than 5,000 francs ($1,000) in bonds, an empty jewel case, and some brass buttons. The Humberts had fled to Madrid but were brought back, tried, and sentenced to five years hard labor. On their release they vanished and the huge scandal, embarrassing for much of upper-class French society, was completely hushed up.

THE BANK EXAMINER

A classic con that is as popular today as ever, this scam has many subtle permutations. The essential element is the mark's unquestioning trust of authority, making elderly people favorite victims.

The Set-Up

1. In the most straightforward form of the scam, the con artist simply waits outside a bank dressed as a police officer or in a suit. Spotting a suitable mark – ideally an elderly lady – coming out of the bank, the con artist approaches her and discreetly asks if he can have a word.

2. In more elaborate set-ups, the con artist gets hold of the mark's name, address, phone number, and as many of their bank details as possible. He then calls the mark and does his pitch over the phone.

3. The con artist flashes a badge of some sort and explains that he is a bank examiner (or any other relevant-sounding law enforcement officer) investigating a case of bank fraud being perpetrated by one of the bank tellers. This will be the teller the mark has just visited (or, if pre-arranged by phone, the one she's instructed to visit). He needs the mark's help. Has she just withdrawn some cash from the bank?

4. The mark reveals that she has, at which point the con artist explains that the teller is passing forged bills (and pocketing the real stuff), and he needs to check hers. Shockingly, it turns out to be forged cash.

The Sting

5. "Just as I feared," the con artist says, "I'm afraid I need to impound this as evidence, but don't worry, you will be refunded by the bank." The mark is reassured and happy at having done her civic duty.

The Players
a. The Con Artist
(possibly in disguise)
b. The Mark

6. If the con man is running a short con, he produces an official-looking receipt. "Take this inside and show it to the manager, he will reimburse you for the impounded money." The mark goes back into the bank and the con disappears.

7. If playing the long con, the con artist explains that to catch the crooked teller in a major violation or a federal crime, he must be caught passing a minimum number of forged bills – usually about $5,000. Will the mark assist in this important and major fraud investigation? There could be a reward in it.

8. If the mark agrees she is sent back into the bank with instructions to visit the same teller as last time and withdraw the cash, but not to tell anyone for fear of tipping him off. She then hands over the large sum and gets a receipt for the full amount.

Variations
The Forged Note Examiner scam is a closely related short con. It involves visiting a store or bar, flashing bogus credentials and asking to examine the contents of the cash register. Of course, forged bills are found and the money must be impounded in return for a receipt.

The Railroad Hustlers:
Gamblers and card sharps

Between the 1850s and 1890s a ragtag brethren of gamblers, hustlers, and short-con masters worked America's riverboats, railroads, army camps, railway laborers and racecourses, practicing classic scams like the Three-Card Monte and the Shell game. Two of the greatest cons of this era were George Devol and Canada Bill Jones.

Canada Bill was born in England but emigrated to Canada, where he became an expert at the Three-Card Monte. His trademark approach was to play the rube – the hopelessly green country boy who was, it appeared, ripe for the taking. Working the riverboats in the South, Canada Bill hooked up with George Devol, one of the great nineteenth-century gamblers and card sharps. In his autobiography, *Forty Years a Gambler on the Mississippi*, Devol describes Canada Bill: "He had a squeaking, boyish voice, awkward, gawky manners, and a way of asking fool questions and putting on a good natured grin, that led everybody to believe that he was the rankest kind of a sucker – the greenest sort of a country jake. Woe to the man who picked him up, though."

Devol was born in Ohio in 1929 and had worked on the riverboats from childhood, observing the flamboyant and charismatic gamblers and learning all their tricks. Where Canada Bill was medium-sized and pretty harmless-looking, Devol was large and particularly famous for his amazingly thick skull, which he was fond of using in fights, and which probably saved his life on numerous occasions when angry marks cracked him over the the head. Devol and Canada Bill made a fortune on the riverboats before the Civil war and then moved onto to the new railroads.

Name: George Devol
Nationality: American/British-Canadian
Years as a con: 40+
Amount earned: $2M+
Years in jail: Unknown

At first they tagged along with the railroad workers laying lines across the country, together with the traveling circus of prostitutes, entertainers, and gamblers known as Hell-on-Wheels. Later they would travel back and forth on the railroads themselves, working the trains for all they were worth. At one point Canada Bill wrote to the head of Union Pacific offering a generous sum for sole rights to practice the Three-Card Monte on his line, and promising to target only Chicago businessmen and Methodist preachers. But the railroads soon cracked down and even started employing detectives to clean up the trains.

By this time both men had made their fortunes, but they spent as quickly as they earned. Canada Bill in particular had a weakness for a popular card game called Faro, "the only game in town."

Canada Bill died, penniless, in Reading, Pennsylvania, in 1880 and was buried in a pauper's grave, although his gambling buddies later clubbed together to pay for his funeral. Devol finally retired in 1886 and wrote his autobiography. Despite having made over $2 million from gambling and card sharping, in 1903 he, too, died broke.

THE JAMAICAN SWITCH

Also known as the Spanish Handkerchief, Country Boy, or the Lottery Scam, the Jamaican Switch is a prototypical con game, closely related to the Pigeon Drop (see page 62). Favorite marks are priests or people of the same ethnic background as the con man.

The Set-Up

1. The con artist, dressed as a poor but honest foreigner, possibly carrying a suitcase, picks his mark – someone kind-looking who will help a foreigner in need, such as a priest.

2. The con artist approaches the mark and asks his help in finding a bank, lawyer, or a cheap hotel. He doesn't speak English very well, but may be carrying a slip of paper with a bogus address for such a hotel.

3. The con artist explains that he is a foreigner who has come into a large sum of American money – an inheritance, perhaps – and he is either looking for somewhere to stay, or is about to leave the country but cannot take the money with him due to currency controls.

4. The con flashes his mich roll, letting the mark see a considerable wad of "cash." Can the mark suggest either a suitable place to stay or help give the money to a worthy cause in return for a share of it?

5. Often there will be a cap involved and he will show up now, posing as a passing ordinary Joe. He will warn the "foreigner" against flashing his money around and advise putting it in a bank. The con artist will protest that he doesn't trust banks, unless the kindly mark can suggest a place.

6. The mark is now asked to produce some "good faith" money, to show that he can be trusted because he has money of his own, or that his bank is trustworthy. Between $2,500 and $5,000 is the usual sum.

The Players
a. The Con Artist
b. The Accomplices
(the cap, capper or shill)
c. The Mark

The Sting
7. The con artist produces a large handkerchief (hence the name) or bag and puts both his mich roll and the good faith money in it. He ties it up and gives it to the mark, for safe-keeping or to "donate" to charity.

8. In fact the con artist has switched the tied-up handkerchief or bag for a ringer containing only shredded newspaper. An opportunity to do this is found by showing the mark how to carry the stash up a sleeve or hidden in an armpit for security.

9. The con artist and mark part company. The mark gets home and opens the package to discover that he's been had.

Variations
A similar con is the Country Boy, where the con artist is a rube from out of town and the mich roll represents his life's savings. In the classic con, the rube is in town looking for a good time and the cap takes him off to visit a prostitute, apparently leaving his stash of money in the hands of the mark, supposedly along with the "good faith" money that proves the mark's trustworthiness.

Ben Marks: Founder of the Big Store

Name: Benjamin Marks
Nationality: American/British-Canadian
Years as a con: 52
Amount earned: $Millions
Years in jail: 0

Ben Marks invented the Big Store con. So influential was he in the world of cons and swindles that some authorities claim his name to be the root of the word still used for the victim of a con game.

Marks was born in Little Fort (now Waukegan), Illinois, in 1848, serving in the army during the Civil War, then making his way westward to Cheyenne, Wyoming, one of the railway boomtowns. In 1867, Cheyenne was the epitome of the Hell-on-Wheels set-up that drew con men and hustlers from all over the west.

Marks's line was the Three-Card Monte, and like many "broad tossers" played the con on a board worn slung around his shoulders, allowing a quick getaway. Marks was good but the competition was stiff, so with the help of a few confederates, he set up what was known as a Dollar Store. This has since become famous as the Big Store con, adapted and perfected in later years by con men such as "Yellow Kid" Weil (see page 122). The Dollar Store was a respectable-enough-looking shop advertising a range of products in the window for just a dollar apiece, even though they were clearly worth more. Once lured inside, the unwary sucker was confronted with a mini-casino of monte games on barrels, and the persuasive patter of Marks and company drew everyone in. Since no one had any money left, no one ever bought the underpriced items and Marks never lost any money.

He was so successful that he built up a tidy sum, and unlike his friends such as Canada Bill and George Devol, he didn't blow it, partly due to his formidable wife Mary, whom he married in 1882. The couple settled in a boomtown in Council Bluffs, Iowa, and set about building themselves a minor empire. Marks ran a Big Store operation in a building which inexplicably had a reputation for being a "square house" – a gambling den where gamblers would not be cheated – even though the games of Monte, Faro, and others were inevitably rigged. Mary, meanwhile, ran the best brothel in town. Between them they made lots of money and reinvested it in Council Bluffs, becoming major players in the social and political establishment.

Ben Marks employed teams of ropers to pick up railroad workers, traveling businessmen, speculators, and other passing suckers, and direct them to his operations. Eventually the Marks built a considerable casino and brothel known as Hog Ranch. Legend has it that it was built across the county line so if there was a raid the patrons could simply move into the next room, on the other side of the border.

In 1913 a tornado damaged much of the Marks empire, and an increasingly unwell Ben ceded control of his operations to the Mabray Gang, a bunch of roughs and swindlers who soon brought the law down on their heads. Ben escaped conviction but died five years later at the age of 71, a well-respected pillar of the community.

THE MUSTARD SQUIRTER

The Players
a. The Con Artist
(usually a woman)
b. The Accomplice (optional)
c. The Mark

This classic and very simple street con involves pickpocketing – a minor deviation from the true grifter's rule that the only tool necessary to scamming is confidence.

The Set-Up

1. The con artist or her accomplice spots a suitable mark. Ideally this will be someone obviously rich and well dressed in an expensive overcoat with a visible wallet bulge.

2. One of them surreptitiously squirts mustard, ketchup, or any other sauce or messy substance down the mark's back.

3. The con artist casually walks past the mark but then stops short and says helpfully, "Excuse me, but did you know that you've got mustard all down your back?"

The Sting

4. The mark is dismayed to discover that this is true but charmed when the kindly lady, obviously an able housewife who knows how to deal with such things, produces some tissues or other suitable props and offers to help clean up the mess: "Take off your jacket for a second and let me have a look at it." (It is not necessary for the mark to take off his coat, but does make the next step easier.)

5. The con artist makes a show of cleaning off the mess while surreptitiously picking the pockets of the coat. "There, now, that's the worst of it off."

6. She sends the mark on his way with exhortations to take the coat to a dry-cleaner, and makes off with her loot.

SCAMS ON SCREEN

CATCH ME IF YOU CAN (2002)

Star rating: ***
Director: Steven Spielberg
Starring: Leondardo Di Caprio, Tom Hanks
Cons: Apart from the ambitious impersonation scams, the film also features paper-kiting or check-hanging, and other forms of forgery. Based on the true story of Frank Abagnale (page 26).

MATCHSTICK MEN (2003)

Star rating: ***
Director: Ridley Scott
Starring: Nicolas Cage, Sam Rockwell
Cons: "Advance fee" prize scams by telephone, where the mark must pay an advance fee to claim a non-existent prize. It also features a badge-play comeback and a version of the Jamaican Switch (page 72).

THE PEDIGREE PET SCAM

One of "Yellow Kid" Weil's favorite hustles, the Pedigree Pet con is a latter-day version of the Fiddle Game (see Variations). Weil estimated that he made more than $7 million from this scam alone. As with all the best cons, it's the mark's own greed that sucks him into the trap.

The Set-Up

1. The con artist acquires a pet, possibly by stealing a smart-looking animal from a front yard. "Yellow Kid" Weil used to pick up a stray mongrel, but somebody's pet probably makes for more convincing bait.
2. The pet is carefully brushed and preened with a collar and ribbons.
3. Pet in hand, the con artist enters a diner and sits at the bar. He strikes up conversation with the barman, who mentions the cute animal, and the con artist extols the virtues and pedigree of his four-legged companion.
4. The con artist explains that he has a business meeting around the corner, dropping hints that it could be a make-or-break-type deal. Would it be OK to leave the pooch with the bartender for a half-hour or so?
5. No sooner has the con artist left than his accomplice enters and sits at the bar, immediately noticing the dressed-up dog. "My God!" he exclaims to the bartender, "What a beautiful animal – a rare pedigree, if I'm not mistaken. How much would it take to get you to part with it?"
6. The bartender explains that the dog isn't his to sell. The cap presses him, offering $500 or more, and settles for a promise that the bartender will pass on his card (proclaiming him to be a breeder or rare pet dealer) and generous offer to the owner when he returns. He is even willing to leave a deposit of $50. Naturally, the cap can never hang around quite long enough to meet the owner himself. Eventually he leaves.

The Players

a. The Con Artist

b. The Accomplice (the cap)

c. The Mark

d. The Mutt

The Sting

7. A few minutes after the cap has left, the con returns, looking downbeat. Ordering a neat double he confesses that the deal fell through and now he is so broke he can only just afford to pay for the drink. The bartender offers a solution. He will buy the dog! How much he offers depends on how much he is willing to "fleece" the con artist for. If he offers $150, he is entirely confident of making a $450 profit by simply ringing the number on the card he's been given.

8. Reluctantly the con artist agrees, takes his money and leaves. The bartender makes the call, only to discover that there's no such number, and that he's just paid $100 or more for a dog he doesn't want.

Variations

In its classic form, the Fiddle Game, this scam was pulled with a cheap violin. The con artist was a down-at-heel busker unable to pay for his dinner, the mark was the restaurant owner or a fellow diner, and the cap was an instrument dealer who would spot that the busker's fiddle was actually a Stradivarius worth many thousands.

THE LOTTERY SCAM

This ruse is still popular today, particularly among America's Latino community, giving rise to its more common name, the Hispanic Lotto Scam. It is essentially a variation on the Pigeon Drop (see page 62).

The Set-Up

1. The con artist picks out the mark on the basis of shared ethnic background. This con works best in ethnic communities with a recent and ongoing history of illegal immigration. Sharing a linguistic and cultural background with the con artist makes the mark more trusting.

2. The con artist approaches the mark looking confused and a little anxious, and asks for help locating a lawyer. He may have the name of a (non-existent) firm on a scrap of paper.

3. At this point the cap approaches and joins in the conversation, wanting to know why the con artist needs a lawyer.

4. The con artist reveals that he needs a lawyer's help to cash in a winning lottery ticket (in fact, the con artist may simply skip straight to this point as step 1). The ticket itself may be a forgery altered to show the winning numbers for extra conviction. The con artist admits that he is an illegal immigrant and dare not cash in the ticket himself for fear of deportation.

5. The cap advises against using a lawyer – they can't be trusted – they love to rip off honest Hispanics. Why not let him cash in the ticket on the con artist's behalf?

The Sting

6. The con has a better idea; why not sell the ticket to the cap and mark? It's worth X thousand dollars – he'll take half, or a fraction of that.

The Players

a. The Con Artist

b. The Mark

c. The Accomplice (the cap)

Alternatively, the con artist will agree with the cap's suggestion but introduce the notion of "good faith" money. He will make sure to appear to be protecting the mark's interests versus the cap – with a ploy something along the lines of: "This gentlemen was kind enough to help me out and now I think it is only fair that he should share in the proceeds . . ."

7. The cap agrees to pay half the asked-for total – usually around $5,000. The mark usually readily agrees to cough up the other half ($2,500). The cap generously allows the mark to hold the ticket and go and cash it in. While the mark is discovering that the ticket is bogus, the other two make good their escape.

Variation

Another scam involving the lottery has recently become a big problem in the UK. Unsuspecting marks receive convincing letters from Canadian PO box addresses, telling them that they've won the Canadian State Lottery and that they only need to pay an advance fee or charge for their prizes to be released.

Serge Stavisky: The man with no face

Name: Serge Alexandre Stavisky
Nationality: Russian
Years as a con: 25+
Amount earned: $40M
Years in jail: 1

Serge Alexandre Stavisky was a mysterious and corrupt figure whose illicit career and suspicious death in 1934 undermined the French establishment and brought the country to the brink of Civil war.

Born in the Ukraine in 1888, Stavisky emigrated to France and began an undistinguished career on the fringes of the law. He went through a succession of jobs, including singing in cafés, managing a night club, nude show, gambling den, and even a soup kitchen. None of them went well but he built up a network of contacts and protectors, possibly thanks to copious bribes.

Soon Stavisky graduated onto more serious scams, based around a state-run pawn shop in the town of Bayonne, in Southwest France. He would issue fake bonds using the pawn shop as security, and is believed to have raised a fortune in this way. There were several attempts to investigate him, but as the scale of his fraud increased so did the profile of his protectors. His network of top policemen, corrupt judiciary officials, and government officials reached almost to the top of the government and he was able to evade prosecution for many years.

By now Stavisky was rich and moved in the most exalted circles of French society. He had a beautiful trophy wife named Arlette along with several mistresses. But what was considered most remarkable about him was how unremarkable he was. He was a tall, pale, nondescript man without a flashy personality, who nevertheless seemed to pull powerful strings in French society. Stavisky's facelessness paid off for a while but eventually he was brought to court. The trial was postponed and delayed for seven years, and Stavisky continued to operate his crooked empire while out on bail, which was scandalously renewed 19 times. But the dance could not go on indefinitely and on January 3, 1934, Serge Stavisky was found shot dead.

With Stavisky's death his highly placed protectors must have breathed a sigh of relief, but the worst was yet to come for them. There was a outcry at the prospect that the corruption that had sustained his career might never come to light. This turned to violent outrage when the Prime Minister refused to sanction an inquiry into the matter, since his brother-in-law was head of the Paris prosecutors' office that had failed in its dealings with Stavisky. French left- and right-wing groups alike seized on the opportunity to score points off the establishment, organizing mass demonstrations that turned into riots. The Prime Minister was forced to resign.

Eventually the public situation calmed down but the scandal continued. A judge who claimed to have secret documents relating to the case was found dead on a railway line – decapitated by a passing train. When Stavisky's associates were finally brought to trial in 1935, 270 witnesses were called, but the double mystery of Serge Stavisky's death and the whereabouts of his ill-gotten gains were never resolved.

MONEY FOR GAS

Panhandling is probably the most common short con or street hustle in the world. Almost everyone has encountered, if not actually fallen for, this scam at some point in their lives.

The Set-Up

1. The panhandler, dressed quite smartly, looking respectable and trustworthy, approaches the mark. The mark may be out and about, working in a shop, or simply sitting around at home.

2. The panhandler explains how embarrassing this is. He's never done anything like this before, he wouldn't be asking if it weren't so urgent, the whole thing sounds ridiculous but . . . etc. This pitch is intended to counteract, from the off, the mark's suspicion that he's being had.

3. The panhandler explains that he is a businessman, teacher, or college professor from out of town, in the city for the day to attend an interview or meeting. Thanks to a rotten stroke of luck his wallet has been lost, stolen, or locked in the car. He can't get home because he's run out of gas, or his car is locked in the parking lot and he can't afford to get it out, or he can't afford his ticket home – because, of course, he's lost his wallet. The details can be vary widely but the essence is always the same.

The Sting

4. "Here's the thing," the panhandler rounds off, "I really need to borrow $20 to pay for gas/redeem my parking ticket/pay my train fare. If you can see your way, out of the goodness of your heart, to lend me the money, I swear I will mail it back to you as soon as I get home this evening. Look, we'll swap addresses, I'll take down your details . . ."

The Players
a. The Con Artist (the panhandler)
b. The Mark

5. Of course most marks, at this point, will be very suspicious, but the con lays it on thick: "I know this sounds dodgy, but I'm honestly telling the truth, I swear it. I wouldn't believe me, either, if I was you, but all I can do is promise you that I'm not lying and that you can trust me. Please will you help me out?" The panhandler is relying on several thought processes running through the mark's head simultaneously. One is the desire to believe that this is their chance to do a good deed and that it is possible to trust a perfect stranger. Second is their fundamental faith in human nature – no one could be such a creep as to swear so vehemently to be telling the truth, while in fact lying barefacedly, could they? Third is the knowledge that they could easily find themselves in a similar position one day, in which case they would hope for some simple human charity. Fourth is the conviction that even a con artist wouldn't go to such lengths for a lousy twenty bucks.
6. Most marks will be overcome by these rationalizations and agree to lend the money. The panhandler makes a big show of writing down the mark's name and address and leaves the mark glowing with self-satisfaction at having helped a fellow human being in need.

THE SPANISH PRISONER

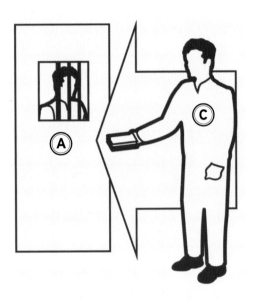

The Players
a. The Con Artist
b. The Accomplices (the contact man, the insider, caps or block hustlers)
c. The Mark

More recently known as the Mexican Prisoner, this scam dates back to Elizabethan times. Still practiced today, it hooks gullible dupes with its unlikely but romantic backstory and promise of fantastic rewards.

The Set-Up
1. The mark receives a letter from the con artist explaining the story, or is befriended by the con artist directly. The letter is written by a wealthy businessman who is currently imprisoned in Mexico. In the original version, the prisoner was a Spanish grandee marooned in Britain after the disastrous Armada expedition. The prisoner has a fortune (usually $250,000 to $500,000) stashed away in America. If the mark can help to secure the prisoner's freedom, half of the loot will be his.
2. In an alternative version, the key to unlock the secret stash of cash, together with bearer bonds for $25,000, is hidden in the false bottom

of a steamer trunk currently held by Mexican customs. Just to sugar the pill a little more, the scam usually includes the prisoner's pretty 18-year old daughter, who must be looked after (and who knows where the loot is hidden). A photo of the winsome beauty completes the picture.

3. The mark is told that cash is needed, either to bribe the guards to secure the prisoner's release, or to secure the release of the impounded steamer trunk. Up to $10,000 is requested.

The Sting

4. In the simplest form of the scam, the grifter convinces the mark of the story and agrees to transfer the bribe money to the corrupt guards. As a block hustle, the mark is told that he must not tell the authorities about the bribe money as this will ruin the plan. The grifter makes off with the cash and the mark will even cover up for him if the police come around.

5. Most marks are too wary for this, so a far more elaborate con is put in motion. The mark is lured to Mexico and taken through a series of meetings with the contact man and, eventually, the insider – an accomplice masquerading as a guard or custom's official. An atmosphere of secrecy is built up to make the mark jumpy and create a block hustle.

6. The con is deadlined by telling the mark that the vital steamer trunk is about to be auctioned off as unclaimed luggage. The mark must quickly hand over the $10,000 needed to settle the impound fees and pay off the various bribes, fines, and court costs.

7. To get rid of the mark completely he is given a bogus key and bearer bonds, and told that the guard has successfully liberated them from the trunk and smuggled them out of the customs office, but now the authorities are closing in and he must flee. The mark flies back to the States to meet the beautiful daughter and open the vault full of money, only to find that they don't exist and he's been elaborately duped.

THE LOADING BAY SCAM

The Players
a. The Con Artist
(the inside man)
b. The Accomplice (the
roper or steerer)
c. The Mark(s)

Also known as the
Delivery Truck or
Truckload scam, in this
hustle the mark is duped
into actually delivering
the money to the hustler.
It trades on the near-
universal desire to get an
"inside" deal or special
trade price.

The Set-Up

1. The roper telephones the shipping department of a company –
preferably a delivery company – and claims to be calling from a large
"white goods" firm that does regular business with them. The firm will
be a reputable one. As they've been such good customers in the past, the
firm wants to show their appreciation by offering them a special deal on
an end-of-year stock clearance (or simply the regular trade price available
only to insiders). On offer are all sorts of high-value goods, including

refrigerators, ovens, high-definition TVs, DVD-players, etc.

A price list guaranteed to command attention is quoted. The deal is only available to bulk purchasers, so does the shipping employee want to pass the word around and gather orders?

2. Alternatively, the roper can make contact with a mark directly, in a bar or other setting. Striking up a conversation, the roper boasts of the amazing deal he just got on a piece of electrical equipment – for example, getting the latest computer for a fraction of the normal price. Nothing illegal about it, he hastens to add, but he knows a guy who works for this delivery company and can get a special price. If the mark's interested he doesn't mind hooking the two of them up to make a deal.

3. After allowing a little while for the mark to gather orders and money, the roper makes contact again, and further instructions are given to the mark. The mark should arrange for one of his firm's trucks (or a hire truck) to come to the loading bay at the warehouse of the reputable firm, where the inside guy will meet him and he can pick up the goods. Remember, the mark is admonished, this deal is "off the books" and unofficial, so it's a cash-only affair.

The Sting

4. The mark shows up at the store front, where he is met by the inside man. The inside man collects the mark's money and, to add an extra layer of conviction, writes him an official-looking receipt (on headed notepaper lifted from an unattended desk), before instructing him to take the truck around back to loading bay X, while he goes inside to open the loading bay doors.

5. The mark drives round to the back of the store to the loading bay area described, and discovers that no one knows what he's talking about. The inside man, meanwhile, flees with the cash.

"Count" Victor Lustig:
The man who sold the Eiffel Tower

Count Lustig was probably Europe's greatest ever con man, remarkable for having successful careers on both sides of the Atlantic.

Victor Lustig was born in Prague in 1890. He was smooth, suave, and sophisticated and fluent in several languages; the very model of a good con man. In later life he came up with "Ten Commandments" of swindling, most of which revolved around the need to be personable and charming, but not too personable or charming. Let the other man speak, be a good listener, and at all times project an air of quiet authority and dignity – these were his hallmarks and they served him well.

Lustig spent some of his early career working the luxury cruise liners between Europe and America, where rich, bored travelers offered fertile ground for suitably smooth con men. In 1925 in Paris he hit upon the idea for one of the most brazen scams in history. At that time the future of the Eiffel Tower was still in doubt. It had been erected as a temporary structure for the 1889 Paris Exposition and many still considered it an eyesore. After reading an article about how much it was costing to maintain, and how run down it was becoming, Lustig realized that, with the right set-up, he could convince people that it was for sale.

With the help of forged documents and stationery, he posed as a government minister and invited six leading scrap merchants to a meeting at an expensive hotel, where he let them in on a "secret." The government was inviting bids for the scrapping of the Eiffel Tower, in what would be a lucrative and prestigious project. Lustig even took them on a chauffeur-driven tour of the Tower. Having picked out his mark, he

Name: Victor Lustig
Nationality: Hungarian
Years as a con: around 20
Amount earned: $Millions
Years in jail: 12

took the scam to its next level by admitting that he was conducting the deal in an underhand fashion because he needed a bribe. A scrap dealer named Andre Poisson fell for his story and handed over a suitcase of money for the bid and the bribe. Lustig hotfooted it out of Paris, but was bemused when no word of the fraud reached the newspapers. Poisson, like so many fraud victims then and now, was simply too embarrassed to admit to having been scammed. Lustig returned to Paris and attempted to repeat the whole scam.

By the 1930s Lustig was plying his trade in America, duping investors with a device called the Fabulous Money Box. To use it, you simply fed a dollar bill and some blank pieces of paper into the machine, waited a day, and then cranked out several perfectly valid copies. Of course the machines were fakes, with hidden drawers that concealed extra bills, but credulous marks snapped them up for as much as $46,000 a go.

Lustig pulled other scams, even crossing swords with the legendary gangster Al Capone at one point, but finally ran out of luck in 1935 when a counterfeiting scam went wrong, landing him in jail, where he died twelve years later.

THE ROCK IN THE BOX

The Players
a. The Con Artist
b. The Mark

This is the original block hustle, and, like the Loading Bay scam, this con trick trades on the average punter's desire to get something for practically nothing. Scams like this allow con artists to justify their crimes on the basis that people get what they deserve.

The Set-Up

1. The con artist sets out his goods in the trunk of a car or pick up. In it are a number of cardboard boxes still in their plastic wrapping, apparently containing high-value items such as DVD-players or televisions.

2. A passing mark is attracted by the con artist's chat – can he really be offering quality goods at such low, low prices (for example, $100 for a $400 item)? How does the mark know what's really in those boxes?

3. The con artist tears open the wrapping on one and opens it up to reveal the item as promised, complete with packaging and instructions. Alternatively, the con artist has several open boxes and sample bits of equipment already on display.

The Sting

4. The mark agrees to purchase the item, even though he knows it's almost certainly stolen goods. In the true block hustle the grifter makes it clear that he is selling "hot" merchandise.

5. In return for his $100 the mark gets a properly printed box, all sealed in plastic that looks and weighs like the real thing. When he gets home and opens it he discovers there's nothing but rocks inside. He's unlikely to complain because then he'd have to admit he was trying to purchase stolen goods.

6. In a more elaborate set-up, such as when selling to a whole crowd of people at once, the con artist may have accomplices who stage a button (a fake police raid) if one of the marks looks like he's about to open his rock-filled ringer. This disperses the crowd pretty quickly and can even give the con artist an escape route as he is "taken into custody."

SCAMS ON SCREEN

OCEAN'S ELEVEN (2001)

Star rating: ***
Director: Steven Soderbergh
Starring: George Clooney, Brad Pitt, Matt Damon
Cons: The main ploy is an elaborate Big Store con, but other scam elements include advance men, inside men, a button, putting on the dog, ringers, and block hustle.

THE COLOR OF MONEY (1986)

Star rating: ****
Director: Martin Scorsese
Starring: Tom Cruise, Paul Newman
Cons: Pool hustle where the con man pretends to be a country jake in order to drive up the odds, then revealing his true skill. Paul Newman's motto is that "you have to be a student of human moves".

Heart, Body, and Soul

The needier a person is, the more gullible they are likely to be. People who desperately want to hear something will do half the con artist's work for him, by convincing themselves that his pitch is true and hearing only what they want to hear. In other words, a needy mark is a good mark, and this is why the scams in this chapter are so successful; scams concerned with emotional, spiritual, or physical need.

Scams that target the lovelorn and desperate are possibly the cruellest cons of all. The unfortunate mark is not only left with an empty bank account but a broken heart and the betrayal of the most complete trust it is possible to place in another person. For this reason, the victims of romantic cons are often the most unwilling to admit they've been conned.

Equally rotten is the con artist who trades on ill health and the need for a cure. However, quackery is so widespread and acceptable today that it is rarely recognized as such, and billions are spent on fad diets, bogus therapies, and spurious treatments every year. The quack's claims resemble the pitches of the "snake oil salesmen" of yesteryear who sold "tonics" and "potions" promoting them with great claims and pseudo-scientific jargon, when they were actually made up of water or alcohol. The supernatural also makes rich hunting grounds for con artists because they depend on faith rather than evidence, and what is faith but a form of confidence? In Victorian times, mediums could become rich by convincing wealthy patrons of their amazing powers. Today a successful fortune teller can expect to make $500,000 a year on average by bilking gullible clients.

THE SWEETHEART SCAM

The Players
a. The Con Artist
b. The Accomplices
c. The Mark

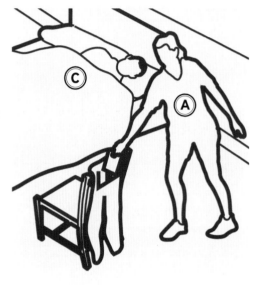

The ultimate scam – making someone fall in love with you. But there is nothing more emotionally painful than betrayal by someone you care about and trust. The victim loses her friend, her belief in humanity, and her money. The ruthless con artist intent on this type of scam frequents places where lonely or widowed women may visit, such as singles clubs or social groups. The Sweetheart Scam is also an umbrella term for any con involving a false romantic or sexual relationship, including the Badger Game and the Panel Game.

The Set-Up
1. The con artist selects and sizes up the mark. This may mean simply spotting a single girl or guy at the bar, or scanning the personal ads columns for likely prospects. Con men and women often target wealthy but lonely widows or widowers by scanning the obituary columns and discovering who has recently been left alone with lots of money.

2. The con artist makes the acquaintance of the mark, possibly using a winning opening line. Sigmund Engels, dubbed "the love pirate" for his exploits from the 1920s to 1940s, used to tell a woman that she looked just like his dear-departed wife, a line that both signaled attraction and attracted sympathy. He also used to dress immaculately and expensively, and let slip that he was a wealthy movie producer.

3. Using all his or her reserves of charm, the con artist wins the affections of the mark often by plying them with the type of flattery and attention that many lonely people crave. This is easier when it is possible to make any number of promises without worrying about having to fulfill them.

The Sting

4. If playing the Badger Game, the con artist lures the poor, unsuspecting mark up to the bedroom and into bed. At this point an enraged husband or father would appear and demand some sort of recompense for having dishonored his spouse or daughter. This type of scam is less likely to work in the modern day.

5. If playing the Panel Game, the hapless mark would be lured into bed and, while he was asleep or otherwise occupied, a secret panel in the wall of the room would be slid back to allow the con artist's accomplice to steal the mark's wallet or other valuables.

6. In a Sweetheart Scam, the con artist may ask for money to help with medical bills, or as an investment in a great new business opportunity. Sigmund Engels would tell his marks that he wanted to set up joint bank accounts for them, and therefore needed access to their money. He would also take their jewelry to be evaluated and re-insured, and then never come back.

7. Once the mark has been milked dry, the con artist moves on to another town and another mark.

HEALTH AND BEAUTY

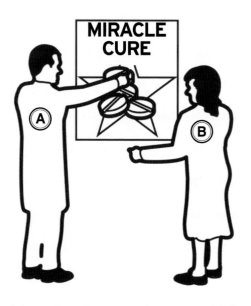

MIRACLE CURE

The Players
a. The Con Artist
(the quack, AKA health guru,
dietician, scientist)
b. The Mark
c. The Advertising Media
(newspapers, magazines,
television)

Dodgy health and beauty products and treatments have been a mainstay of the con industry since the snake oil salesmen (see page 94) and traveling quacks of the eighteenth and nineteenth centuries. Today they are even more prevalent – you can find half a dozen simply by turning to the complementary and alternative medicine section of any monthly magazine.

The Set-Up

1. The quack surveys the current state of science and medicine and assesses the most common public health or beauty concerns of the day. By combining the two, he can invent a product or therapy that meets a need in a way that the general public will find plausible. The most favored areas are those perceived by the layman as cutting-edge but also incomprehensible – classic examples include electromagnetism, quantum physics, vibrations, and radioactivity. More recently, with the increasing public appetite for "natural" rather than "artificial" substances, quacks are focusing more on rare herbal preparations and "naturally" sourced vitamins and minerals.

2. The quack prepares an eye-catching pitch to use in publicity material. There are several key pseudoscience strategies common to all such pitches. Buzzwords such as "potentiated" or "microgranules" are used, along with technical or scientific terms and jargon (such as, quantifying supposed results in percentage terms). Authority figures are appealed to, although they may well be bogus – for example, "Validated in tests by Professor Q. Snakeoil of the University of FlimFlam." Adverts will be peppered with glowing testimonials. Anecdotal evidence such as this is meaningless but, more importantly from the quack's point of view, is hard to dispute or prove to be false.

3. The quack buys advertising space in a popular magazine or newspaper or simply fires out millions of spam e-mails.

The Sting

4. Gullible and/or desperate marks send in their checks, money orders, cash, and credit card details in return for the miracle fat-loss cure or cosmetic wonder-working, coral-derived calcium tablet or amazing migraine-relief acupressure bracelet that the quack has advertised. To avoid being accused of mail fraud or simple theft the quack needs to send something back. Usually it will have convincing packaging and may even contain some of the ingredients promised.

5. The quack product will have no intrinsic value, but may produce remarkable results simply by virtue of the placebo effect. A placebo is a physiologically inactive or neutral substance that makes the patient feel better through the power of suggestion.

HALL OF FAME

Dr John Brinkley: The goat-gland surgeon

Name: John Romulus Brinkley
Nationality: American
Years as a con: 20+
Amount earned: $15M+
Years in jail: 0

Doctor, surgeon, sex therapist, talk show host, broadcasting mogul, politician, populist – Dr John Brinkley was all of these and more. John Romulus Brinkley was born into backwoods poverty in 1885, and had an undistinguished early career as a telegrapher, snake oil salesman, and electro-medical quack. After a minor run-in with the law for fraud, he settled in Kansas armed with a $500 MD from the Eclectic Medical University of Kansas City. It was a totally bogus degree, but incredibly, it allowed him to practice legitimately in Kansas.

He got a job as a family doctor in a small town called Milford. One day a local farmer came to see him, complaining of a low libido, and between them they arrived at the preposterous idea that implanting goat glands might rejuvenate his sex drive. Gland transplants were a hot medical topic at the time, with doctors in America and Europe making headlines with their glandular rejuvenation theories. Brinkley cut open the farmer's testicles, implanted a goat gonad and within a week the patient reported success; within a year he had fathered a boy. This unlikely triumph was to lead to great things. Word spread and soon Brinkley had eager suckers beating a path to his clinic door. Brinkley turned the business into a medical production line, keeping a stable of goats out the back to provide the raw material. But the real secret of Brinkley's success was his marketing genius. He played the folksy, down-home doctor role brilliantly, promising sexual potency and claiming that his procedure only failed if the patient was the "stupid type."

In 1923 he hit upon his marketing masterstroke and set up a radio station. KFKB – Kansas First, Kansas Best – was equipped with a powerful transmitter that allowed Brinkley's broadcasts to be heard halfway across the Atlantic. Via his "Medical Question Box" show he operated a scam where he prescribed remedies according to a number-coded system, to be filed at participating pharmacists in the patient's locale. The remedies were nothing more than colored water and the pharmacists paid Brinkley a hefty kickback.

Soon Brinkley ran into trouble with the American Medical Association (AMA) and the federal radio regulators. KFKB was finally closed down in 1931, but Brinkley simply moved to Del Rio, Texas, and bought a new and even more powerful radio station just across the border in Mexico, where regulations were lax. XER was the most powerful radio station in the world. Streams of patients flooded into town and soon Brinkley practically owned Del Rio. By 1937 he had three yachts, a fleet of Cadillacs, and a huge estate where penguins and tortoises roamed free.

In 1939 things started to go wrong. By 1941 he was off the air and bankrupt. He was sued for mail fraud by the Postal Service, and had a stroke that led to his leg being amputated. He died later that year.

FORTUNE TELLERS

Fortune telling, or divination, is one of the oldest professions and has been big business for millennia. The advance of science seems to have made little impression on popular levels of belief in its efficacy.

The Set-Up
1. The beauty of the fortune-telling scam is that the mark comes to the con artist. Apart from saving effort on the con's part, this also means that the most gullible section of the population self-selects. The fact that the mark has turned up guarantees that half the con artist's work is done.
2. If the fortune teller is running a well-established operation, he or she may have proper premises, with a reception room and receptionist. Here the mark may be engaged by a fellow client who is actually a shill, whose job it is to glean any information possible through small talk.
3. If the mark has booked the appointment in advance, the fortune teller and his or her associates have the opportunity to do some background research, via the Internet, local directories, or public records. Every nugget of information gleaned about the mark counts.
4. The mark is shown into the "consulting room" which may be dimly lit and atmospherically decorated. Low lighting and props such as a turban can be handy for concealing communication devices or other tricks the fortune teller can use to receive information from confederates.

The Sting
5. The "consultation" begins the moment the mark walks in and engages in small talk with the fortune teller. Every detail of appearance, body language, and conversation is noted and filed away for possible use.

The Players

a. The Con Artist (AKA the astrologer, tarot reader, crystal-ball gazer, palm reader, scryer, mystic, seer, gypsy, wise woman, psychic, medium, witch, witch-doctor, wizard or medicine man, ju-ju man, channeler, contactee, shaman)

b. The Accomplices (the receptionist, researcher, investigator)

c. The Mark (AKA the client)

6. Using cold reading techniques, the con is able to glean information from the mark while making it appear to have come out of nowhere.

7. If making predictions, the con will keep them general or make specific predictions that have a very high probability of coming true.

8. Expert con artists use their consultations to draw suitable marks into further scams. "Yellow Kid" Weil (see page 120), for instance, was friends with a phoney medium who advised a client that an encounter with a bearded stranger would offer an amazing investment opportunity. A few days later she just happened to run into the bearded Weil . . .

Variations

Some phoney fortune tellers and psychics (see Cassie Chadwick, page 50) would hire a private eye and ferret out dirt on their clients. They would then "discover" the dirt through clairvoyance and blackmail their clients.

Florence Cook and the ghost of Katie King

Florence Cook perpetrated one of the most scandalous séance room frauds of the Victorian era.

The second half of the nineteenth century was the heyday of the medium. Many revealed incredible secrets from "beyond the grave" and claim amazing powers from levitation and clairvoyance to the manifestation of ectoplasm – a sticky substance suspiciously similar to wet muslin that was held to be matter from the spirit dimension. Most of the celebrated mediums were caught out engaging in deception at one point or another, but many people in intellectual and scientific circles believed there might be something in the revelations of spiritualism and were determined to find proof to back it up. Sir William Crookes was one man. A gentlemen scientist of international renown he had investigated one of the most celebrated mediums of the era, Daniel Dunglas Home, coming to believe in the veracity of spiritualism. This made him the perfect mark for Florence Cook, a pretty young medium building a reputation for herself. Cook came from a lower-middle-class East London family who had got involved in mediumship as a way to make money. Public displays could be lucrative as people would pay for the privilege of being "sitters" at a séance, but even better was to win the patronage of a wealthy believer such as Charles Blackburn of Manchester, who was already funding the spiritualist group that had "discovered" Cook. To increase her credibility, Cook began to receive visits from the spirit of Katie King, the daughter of a seventeenth-century pirate. King was a popular visitor to mediums in Europe and America, but Cook managed to actually materialize her "ectoplasmic" form.

Name: Florence Cook
Nationality: British
Years as a con: 4
Amount earned: Unknown
Years in jail: 0

By 1873 Cook was ready to involve Crookes, and approached him to help verify her incredible powers. After a series of supposedly rigorous experiments Crookes declared himself satisfied that there was no trickery involved. During the trials Crookes would be visited by the pretty "spirit," who would sit on his lap and kiss and fondle him in ways quite forbidden to Victorian ladies, but permissible to spirits. He was well aware of the fact that she looked exactly like Cook and seemed to be a living, breathing girl. "The ghost," he reported, "was as material a being as Miss Cook herself." So why did he not put two and two together? Perhaps his infatuation with the charming ghost blinded him to the obvious and led him to overlook the latitude for trickery that was allowed in the séance-room set-up. Cook was allowed to enter a closet, spend a few minutes inside (presumably changing) and then emerge as a "ghost," shutting the curtains behind her.

Whether or not she or her alter-ego King slept with Crookes, Florence Cook got the endorsement she wanted and, duly, the regular allowance from the gullible Mr Blackburn.

FAITH HEALERS

The Players
a. The Con Artist
(AKA the faith healer
or psychic surgeon)
b. The Accomplices
(the shills)
c. The Mark

The process of faith healing is making a comeback thanks to new evangelist movements and it is now reaching larger audiences than ever, due to its televised output. However, it has yet to approach the popularity of its heyday, in turn-of-the-century revival meetings and shows that became big business, drawing in millions.

The Set-Up
1. Faith healing depends on the placebo effect for any effect that it produces, so the faith healer's success is completely dependent on creating the right mood in the mark, and this depends on the pitch. Some faith healers work with a crowd of people, others on a one-to-one basis. The setting determines the pitch.

2. If working with a crowd of people, the faith healer whips them up into a fervour with preaching, singing, and dancing. Sometimes marks will have fasted for long periods or even taken mind-altering substances that will further add to their gullibility.

3. If working one-on-one with the mark, the faith healer needs to exert sufficient personal charisma to make the patient susceptible to suggestibility. This can be done through preaching or by explaining the theory behind the healing process in a similar fashion to the pseudoscientific pitch made for quack cures. For example, "This crystal will realign your positive and negative auras, which I can sense have gone into a state of reversed polarity."

4. Shills may be employed to demonstrate the remarkable curative powers of the faith healer, for example, "miraculously" regaining the power of sight or the use of their legs.

The Sting

5. The precise act of healing depends on the type of faith healer. Evangelistic healers call people up to the stage, using the added pressure of the conformity urge (see page 25) to affect them. The healing process is accomplished simply by touching or smacking the mark on the head. The power of suggestion does the rest.

6. Psychic surgeons use fake blood and sleight of hand to appear to put their hands into the mark's body and remove a piece of tissue (which is actually animal tissue they have previously palmed).

7. Complementary or alternative therapists may use gentler methods such as massage or the laying on of hands. (This is also known today as the therapeutic touch.)

8. Marks who complain about lack of results are told that they have failed through lack of belief.

STAR MAKERS

The Players
a. The Con Artist (AKA the agent, photographer, or producer)
b. Accomplices (the ropers, steerers, or shills)
c. The Mark (AKA the "wannabe")

The growth of celebrity culture has created an ever-increasing tide of "wannabe" celebrities – people who are desperate to become models, actors, singers, or just in the public eye. Where there's demand there's always a ready supply of con artists to cash in. Enter stage left – the star maker.

The Set-Up
1. The con artist puts together a convincing set-up, printing up business cards and other props and possibly even hiring an office and/or studio space to add to the overall effect.
2. The con artist advertises his services in the appropriate media, or mimics the strategies of legitimate talent spotters, using ropers and steerers to approach marks at talent contests or simply out and about (for example, in shopping malls).

3. During his pitch the con artist boasts of his previous successes, of his personal access to potential employers (record companies, magazines, studios, photographers) and of the professional service he can offer. He also talks up the mark's chances of success, praising their wonderful looks, voice, or talent. Skillful con artists know to concentrate their charm on the parents – usually the mother, who is regarded as fairly easy to win over. Finally, the con artist points out what a low percentage he charges in commission – not like those sharks at the larger, more well-known talent agencies that we have all heard about.

4. The mark is given an authoritative-sounding action plan – perhaps to compile a portfolio of shots or put together a demo disc.

The Sting

5. The mark is told that it costs a certain amount of money to put together the portfolio/demo tape/showreel, and is bilked for costs for the photographer, stylist, producer, engineer, studio time, etc. There may also be handling or registration fees. The mark is encouraged to think of this as an investment in his or her career.

6. There are often continued delays and obstacles that can only be overcome by the mark parting with more cash.

7. In the end, the mark may well end up with a shoddy portfolio, demo disc, or showreel to show for their pains, but it is very rare that the promised access or opportunities will materialize.

Variations

The unfortunate starstruck mark may be invited to a phony agency office or recording studio where shills are on hand and are busy looking busy. This step effectively makes the Star Maker con a Big Store scam, like the Wire (see page 114).

HALL OF FAME

Dr Albert Abrams: The father of radionics

Name: Dr Albert Abrams
Nationality: American
Years as a con: 14
Amount earned: $2M+
Years in jail: 0

The key ingredient of any invention or science hoax is the Black Box. This is the mysterious device that performs amazing feats never before achieved, the inner workings of which are a secret known only to the inventor and far too complex to be revealed to the ignorant mark.

No one made more money or sparked more controversy with a Black Box-style gizmo than Dr Albert Abrams, inventor of the Dynamizer and the Oscilloclast, credited by many as being the Father of Radionics.

In practice, radionics – the use of spurious and vague devices to generate or detect electrical and magnetic fields for the diagnosis and treatment of disease – has a long and dishonorable history, dating back to the eighteenth century. Electricity was a natural field for the charlatan, quack, and scientific con man. It was poorly understood by almost everyone, seemed mysterious to the point of being occult, and had been demonstrated as a prevailing force of nature. Ever since Galvani used primitive batteries to animate severed frogs legs, the potential existed for people to be duped by the "healing power of electricity."

Dr Albert Abrams started out as a respectable doctor who quickly climbed to the top of his profession, becoming a pillar of the San Francisco medical establishment. But a few years later he began to develop a strange and self-serving theory of physics modestly titled the Electronic Reactions of Abrams (ERA).

ERA provided the theoretical basis for a strange device that Abrams christened the Dynamizer – an impressive-looking box equipped with dials and lights, much like the new-fangled radio sets of the time, which could be used to diagnose illness in a patient. In the hands of a trained practitioner, the Dynamizer could diagnose illness from a blood sample, a hair, or even a person's handwriting or voice. It "worked" by picking up electronic vibrations emitted by organs afflicted with disease.

Abrams even invented new diseases to be diagnosed by the Dynamizer. To treat the diseases Abrams came up with a device called the Oscilloclast. Eager practitioners flocked to Abrams's clinic for expensive training and to purchase the even more expensive machines, and then went forth to treat the unwary public. By 1921, 3,500 practitioners were using ERA devices. Inevitably mistakes and misdiagnoses followed and the AMA launched a fierce assault on Abrams, but the old doctor had powerful celebrities in his corner, including authors Upton Sinclair and Sir Arthur Conan Doyle. In 1923 fraud cases were launched against some ERA quacks. Abrams was called as the star witness at one trial, but died of pneumonia in January, 1924, worth a reputed $2 million. A Dynamizer was later revealed as nothing but wires, lights, and buzzers. But perhaps he wasn't such a quack after all – using his own device, he had previously diagnosed his own life expectancy, predicting that his death would occur in January, 1924!

Gamblers Anonymous

Gamblers provide the con artist with an obvious and willing pool of potential marks; often it isn't even necessary to cheat, although this is usually involved. Many of the classic angles from the great age of con artists (1850 to 1940) revolved around gambling in some form or another, from the Three-Card Monte (see page 58) of the riverboat gamblers and Railroad Hustlers (see page 70), to the Wire game of "Yellow Kid" Weil (see page 120). Strangely, however, con artists themselves have traditionally been suckers for gambling, with the majority of them losing as much as they ever won in games of chance, crooked or otherwise.

A key element in the gambling con is the "sure thing." This is where the mark is somehow convinced that he can beat the odds – that winning is a dead cert. Invariably this is because he's been duped, but when he loses he can't complain because he was attempting to rip off the con artist. The Three-Card Monte works so well because the mark is allowed to believe he's on to a sure thing. Often a shill will confide in him that the queen is marked in some way, and then prove his point by winning. When the mark tries to follow suit he discovers that somehow the queen has been unmarked and another card marked instead. Other gambling cons include the lemon, where con artists work in a team to bilk the mark in a card game; and the hot seat, where the mark is dealt a killer hand, such as four aces, bets the house, then discovers someone else has a straight flush!

THE WIRE

Also known as the Joint, the Store, the Big Store and the Big Con, this is the classic betting-parlor version of the Big Store con, originated by "Paper Collar" Joe Kratalsky and Christ Tracy in 1898 and perfected by "Yellow Kid" Weil. This con is featured in the movie *The Sting*.

The Set-Up

1. The roper, lugger, or steerer befriends the mark and pitches him a story about how he knows a guy who has inside access to the racing results before they are officially announced. This is hard to pull off today, but around the turn of the last century racing results were telegraphed around the country down the wire. According to the con artists' pitch, they have an inside guy who can tap the wire and/or delay the transfer of results to the betting parlor.

2. The mark is taken to meet the con artist, who in turn takes him to see the supposed inside guy, a cap dressed in the right uniform, at the telegraph offices.

3. Now convinced that he's going to be given the inside information on a big winner, the mark is taken along to a convenient betting parlor. What he doesn't know is that this is a "rig" – an elaborate fake, set up in a temporarily disued hall and peopled with minor con artists and bit-part players busily pretending to be bookies and customers. All the clocks are set slightly fast, so that the con artists genuinely know ahead of the mark which horses are winners and which are losers.

4. The mark may be allowed to win a few small bets, showing that the inside info is for real and convincing him he's on to a sure thing.

5. At the crucial moment the mark is given the nod to bet on a long-odds

The Players
a. The Con Artist
b. The Accomplices (the ropers, luggers, steerers, shills, caps, button men)
c. The Mark

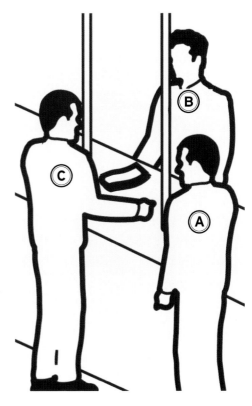

winner. Depending on the exact scam, a cap joins him in going to place a bet.

The Sting
6. In Weil's version of the Wire, the mark is prevented from placing his bet "in time" by a carefully staged diversion, such as a fight. He is then persuaded to cough up some cash to pay off the inside man anyway, and then promptly gulled into entering another con.
7. In the version of the Wire practiced by Fred and Charley Gondorf, the kings of the Big Store con in New York from 1900 to 1915, the supposed "sure thing" fails to win and both the mark and the cap lose their bets.
8. The cap kicks up such a fuss that the mark doesn't feel so bad and/or is distracted from having lost.
9. If things need to be broken up because the mark has a beef, a "button" may be pulled, in which a fake police raid is staged to break up the gathering and scare off the mark.

HALL OF FAME

Oscar Hartzell and the Drake Inheritance

Name: Oscar Merrill Hartzell
Nationality: American
Years as a con: 19
Amount earned: $0.7 to 1.3M
Years in jail: 8

The fake inheritance scam is an old con that still has legs today, but nobody in American history has pulled it off on the scale managed by one-time cattleman Oscar Hartzell.

Hartzell got into the scam through being a victim himself. In 1915, as a down-on-his-luck cattle farmer searching for a lifeline, he fell for a fake investment scam based around a fictional Drake Inheritance. The story was that the Elizabethan admiral and adventurer Sir Francis Drake had left an undisclosed legacy, sure to be worth millions, in captured Spanish bullion, and that his descendants were, to this day, fighting to get the British government to release it. For just a few dollars towards the legal costs, the lucky investor could buy a share in the estate at a rate of return of up to 1000 to one. Hartzell's mother had already invested $6,000, a small fortune at the time, and he too fell for the scam.

Having got wind of the con, Hartzell got involved himself and soon took over the scam entirely, moving to England and using letters, telegrams, and a network of agents back home to recruit suckers throughout the Midwest. He used his farming background to best effect to convince smallholders, shopkeepers, and other ordinary Joes and Joans from Iowa and surrounding areas to cough up a few dollars each. They were promised fabulous returns within just a few weeks, but inevitably, delays kept cropping up.

The "shareholders" were totally taken in. Hartzell arranged meetings in small communities around the Midwest, where local investors would turn up and discuss the progress of the "case" and make plans for how they would spend the thousands of dollars shortly to be paid out. Hartzell turned heads with his wild speculations, promising that the Drake Inheritance was worth $15 million or more. "When I get this money," Hartzell memorably boasted, "I could buy the three states of Missouri, Kansas, and Iowa, put a fence around the whole lot and then have more gold left over than all of you ever dreamed of."

The authorities did everything they could to stop folks falling for the scam, denouncing Hartzell as a fraud and at one point making it illegal to sell shares in the Drake estate. Even when the stock market crashed in 1929 and the Depression hit the Midwest the marks kept sending in their dollars, even more desperate now for that big pay day. Hartzell even claimed that the crash was caused by the impending settlement of the case and the flood of money that would follow.

In 1933, Hartzell was extradited back to Iowa to face charges, but, released on bail, he continued to run his scam and even raised money to pay for his defense. Gullible investors refused to believe that he was scamming them and continued to trust his patter. Their confidence did not prevent him from being found guilty and he was sentenced to 10 years. He died in prison in 1943 with only a dime in his pocket.

MATCH AND THE POT GAME

Gambling cons don't have to be long cons like the Wire. Two short cons are Match (also known as Smack) and the Pot Game. Match was popular around 1900, when it was practiced on marks at train stations. The Pot Game may be found at any bar.

Match

1. The con artist strikes up a conversation with the mark at the train station. They are joined by the cap, playing a real country rube.

2. The con artist gets the cap to play a game of matching coins with him. This involves flipping coins and calling out heads or tails – whomever calls correctly keeps both coins. Because the coins are smacked onto the back of the hand after flipping, the game is also known as Smack.

3. The con artist cheerfully tips the mark a wink and whispers to him, "You call heads and I'll call tails, and that way one of us will always win – we can take this guy for all he's got and split the winnings later."

4. The mark is happy to lose to his new friend because he believes they're both conning the rube.

5. After they've cleaned out the cap (and the mark), the con artist and the mark go off to the diner to split the winnings.

6. The cap shows up at the diner before the split can take place and accuses them of being in cahoots. "I don't mind losing," he says for the benefit of the assembled crowd, "but I ain't gonna be taken for a ride. You fellas'll have to prove you're not together by going your separate ways."

7. The con artist whispers to the mark that they'll have to split up but he'll meet him on the train later, in a particular carriage. The cap watches them to make sure they go off in separate directions.

The Players

a. The Con Artist
b. The Accomplice
(the cap or grifter)
c. The Mark

8. The mark gets on his train, and only when it's pulled out of the station does he realize he's been conned.

The Pot Game

1. The grifter strikes up a conversation with a mark at the bar.

2. After a few drinks (preferably with the mark quite drunk), the grifter suggests a little game. "This is a game where we take it in turn to bid for a pot of money – whoever makes the highest bid gets to buy the whole pot for that amount."

3. The pot consists of $5 from each player. The money is placed in some kind of vessel on the bar.

4. Whatever the mark bids, the grifter always starts off bidding at $5.

5. The mark must then raise the bid if he wants to avoid simply losing his $5. Whatever he bids (for example, $6), wins the game.

6. The grifter admits defeat, giving the $6 with good grace. The mark collects the whole pot, delighted at his good fortune and unaware that he's just been bilked for a dollar (or more, if he bid higher) – he has, of course, just paid $6 to get $5, since one of the fives was his anyway.

The Yellow Kid:
The cartoon-character con artist

Regarded as the greatest con man in US history, Joseph "Yellow Kid" Weil was a true American original. In a crooked career that spanned 60 years, Weil invented innumerable scams and perfected the Big House con, providing the inspiration for the classic 1973 movie, *The Sting*.

Joseph Weil was born in Chicago in 1877, although he later claimed it was 1875 so that he could say he'd lived to be 100. He started at the bottom, working as a shill for a snake oil hustler, helping to part rural rubes from their cash in return for bogus remedies. He graduated to solo scamming in rural areas before returning to the big city with a bundle of cash. It was about this time that he acquired his nickname, "Yellow Kid," after a character in a popular cartoon strip that he liked.

For the next few years Weil exploited the technicalities of betting on the "geegees," as they were in the early 1900s, when results were telegraphed around the country via "the golden wire," a wire service provided by Western Union. Weil and his associates, such as Fred "The Deacon" Buckminster, a crooked Chicago vice cop, would fleece marks in a variety of ways. Often these revolved around a shill planted at the Western Union offices who could be introduced as the inside man, willing to intercept messages from the wire and pass on information before it got to the bookies, so that the mark could then make a bet guaranteed to pay off. In one version of the scam the shill would write the results on a piece of paper and hide it in a rubber ball, which he would toss from the top floor of the Western Union building. The mark would be sent scurrying after the ball as it bounced out of sight.

Name: Joseph Weil
Nationality: American
Years as a con: around 60
Amount earned: $Millions
Years in jail: several

The most famous betting scam that Weil pulled, however, was an elaboration of the Big House con invented by Ben Marks (see page 74). Weil's original version of this, based around a phoney bookmaker's, is now known as the Wire (see page 114).

In later years Weil took his Big House con on the road and moved it up a notch. He would hire out recently vacated banks in small towns and staff them with shills, and use the convincing setting to encourage investors to leave large amounts of cash in his safekeeping. When they returned they would discover just an empty building. Weil honed this ploy to the highest pitch, eventually finding that he could talk real bank managers into lending him their offices for a few hours and then duping the rich mark with a stand-in "bank manager" to the same effect.

Weil tried going straight occasionally but his legitimate business ventures always foundered, largely because of his bad name. He also went to jail twice after being nabbed for holding dodgy bonds, and eventually retired in his seventies, becoming a much-loved local character on the streets of Chicago, where he died in 1976.

White Collar Scams

White collar fraud, including embezzlement, is the most common form of con and also the most profitable. According to a recent estimate, fraud perpetrated against companies by their employees (AKA occupational fraud) costs $600 billion a year in America alone. This doesn't include white collar scams perpetrated against companies and individuals by crooked companies and con artists pretending to be companies.

This chapter looks in detail at some of the most notorious and common white collar scams that the average individual is likely to encounter, but white collar fraud itself runs the gamut from fiddling expenses or minor mis-statement of expenditure in a tax return, to major corporate scandals such as insider trading. Despite the high cost of fraud to companies (accounting for up to 6 percent of revenue), only a tiny proportion of white collar con artists are ever brought to book by the law. The more likely outcome is detection by the company itself, but the skilled white collar scammer knows how to minimize the chances of this happening and are usually careful to observe the following: 1) Don't take vacations. If you are not in the office someone else might be filling in for you, and they might spot some discrepancies or oddities which could "blow the gaff." 2) Don't get greedy. Banks, accountants, and managers are not likely to question small invoices or checks, but eyebrows may be raised over large sums. 3) Don't show off. Suspicions may be raised if a low-paid employee has a new car, or a middle-manager moves into a mansion. 4) Bilk companies that do not have anti-fraud safeguards.

HIGH YIELD INVESTMENT (HYI) FRAUDS

The Players
a. The Con Artist
(the inside man)
b. The Accomplice
(the middleman AKA
the steerer or roper)
c. The Mark

HYI schemes target marks who think that they're too smart to fall for a scam. Housewives to savvy big-businessmen are taken for thousands, dazzled by the promise of returns that are literally too good to be true.

The Set-Up
1. The middleman contacts the mark and pitches by e-mail, letter, or phone. The pitch involves a high-yield investment offering higher rates of return than normal investment methods (savings accounts, bonds, etc). The exact type of HYI varies from the unlikely (bonds recovered from a crashed WWII aircraft in the jungle) to the highly convincing (stock in a biotech company that's about to get federal endorsement).

2. The mark is told that access to the HYI depends on whether he can impress the inside man, who is portrayed as a connected insider who can make people's fortunes.

3. The mark is bamboozled with official-looking certificates, bonds, etc. He is instructed to sign letters of intent, powers of attorney and non-circumvention, non-disclosure agreements, and supply proof-of-funds. All this is presented as necessary to gain access to the inside man.

4. The mark is allowed to make contact with the inside man. The inside man explains that the HYI is only possible because it is not strictly legitimate. Discretion is essential. This puts in place the block.

5. The mark is tapped for initial fees – but not enough to scare them off. Some of this money may be fed back to the mark as "initial profits," feeding their desire to get more involved. In effect, this is a convincer.

The Sting

6. The mark is told that now is the time to strike – he must wire funds to the inside man. If the mark hesitates he is threatened with red-inking – being struck out of the deal and missing out on the opportunity. The deal may also be deadlined as a hurry-up – the mark is told that the window of opportunity is closing fast.

7. The mark is now at the "hurrah" – the point where he is completely committed to the scheme. This allows the con artists to bilk him for more funds to protect his existing investments.

8. As the mark becomes anxious he is stalled with a variety of excuses. The longer he can be held off, the harder it will be for him to recover any money and the easier it is for the con artists to cover their tracks.

9. To forestall the mark complaining to the authorities he is blocked with scare tactics – telling him, for example, that the police are on to the scheme; or that the mark himself is implicated.

Enron: A groundbreaking swindle

Name: Enron
Nationality: American
Years as a con: around 16
Amount earned: $Billions
Years in jail: Various cases still in progress

The collapse of Enron and the scandal that followed marked the end of the long 1990s bull market and the onset of a depression. Crooked CEOs and directors made millions and employees and investors lost billions in a swindle that was groundbreaking in scope but familiar in its method.

Enron started as a fuel supply company in Houston in 1985, concerned solely with supplying gas to buyers. Thanks to deregulation of the power market, it was able to significantly expand and diversify its operations during the 1990s, and Enron's services became highly complex and a little mysterious, but the markets didn't care. The quarterly reports showed ever-improving turnover and the share price kept surging. This was enough to keep fund managers, financial analysts, and investors happy. Enron was touted as the ideal model for an aggressive, fast-moving, and profitable company in the new era of globalization. Enron staff were encouraged to invest in its shares, and rabble-rousing presentations given by senior management encouraged the belief that they were involved in a great enterprise. Unfortunately for employees and investors alike, the men at the top were engaged in shady practices. The basic fraud was the Managed Earnings scam. This is where a company lies about its earnings and manages the books to improve what investors see in the reports that inform their investment decisions. Turnover and profits look good, costs and debts look low. The share price rises and the management, who award themselves large bonuses, can cash in and make millions.

In Enron's case the key elements of the swindle involved putting potential future earnings on the books as current earnings, while hiding debt by shifting it off the Enron balance sheet and into shady partnerships and associate enterprises.

What made the Enron scandal truly appalling to the financial world was that the official auditors, Arthur Andersen (at the time one of the world's top five accountancy firms), whose job it was to guard against precisely this sort of shenanigan, appeared to be complicit. They were soliciting millions in fees and consultancy charges from Enron while also supposedly policing their accounts, and auditors were later accused of shredding documents when the whole fraud started to be exposed.

The exposure happened in 2001 when a company whistleblower raised concerns. A number of investigations began and the stock value plummeted. The directors sold billions of dollars worth of stock but investors and employees lost investments, savings, pensions, and eventually jobs. Arthur Andersen was barred from corporate auditing and is no longer one of the Big Five accountancy firms. Enron stock was eventually delisted from the Stock Exchange.

PYRAMID SCHEMES

The Players
a. The Con Artist
b. The Marks

Probably the best-known form of white collar fraud, the pyramid scheme is currently enjoying a new lease of life thanks to scams such as Circle of Trust and Women Helping Women. The key element is that the marks become the middlemen or ropers.

The Set-Up
1. The con artist sets up the pyramid using e-mail, letters, or local advertising. A meeting of interested parties is arranged at a local venue.
2. The pitch outlines the scheme, but without mentioning giveaway terms such as pyramid. The marks are told that, in order to join the scheme, they must pay a registration fee to the person who recruits them (i.e. the person giving the talk). That person keeps half the fee and passes the other half up the next level of the pyramid (although the pitch is likely to describe this as "the next link in the chain" to obscure the truth). The mark's task is then to "recruit" as many more marks as possible – she gets to keep half of their registration fees, passing the other halves up the

pyramid. If their marks then recruit more people, they will be at the apex of the pyramid, taking in fees from dozens of people.

3. Graphs and diagrams are used to "explain" this and impress the marks. Even more telling are the testimonials from people who assert that they've made thousands of dollars by doing essentially nothing. Modern schemes often dress up the basic scam with empowerment philosophy and even community action drives, such as collecting food tins for charity.

The Sting

4. The marks sign up and cough up their fees – usually in the region of a few hundred dollars. The con artist at the apex of the pyramid rakes in several thousand dollars.

5. The marks go forth and attempts to multiply. Those who get in on the scheme early may succeed, as there will be plenty of untapped marks. But as the number of middlemen grows exponentially, it only takes two or three steps of the pyramid until there are no more marks in the area. Since only the top tiers of the pyramid make any money, 88 percent of marks find that they are out of pocket with no chance of remuneration, while the con artist who set the ball rolling makes off with the loot. Marks who have roped in friends and family may find themselves very unpopular. Entire communities have been ruined in this way.

Variations

Multi-level marketing schemes (MLM), such as the notorious Amway, are essentially pyramid schemes where the middlemen actually have a product to try and sell. As well as selling the product themselves, the real aim is to recruit others as salespeople, who then buy their stock from you, so that you become a wholesaler/supplier as well as a retailer. The most common MLM scams revolve around supplements and cosmetics.

PONZI SCHEMES

Although first practiced in the US by William "520 Per Cent" Miller in 1899, this type of scam, also known as a Peter-to-Paul scam, is named after its most famous practitioner, Charles Ponzi (see page 140). It is sometimes described as a pyramid scheme with only two levels – the con artist and everyone else.

The Set-Up

1. The con artist offers a "unique" investment opportunity with fantastically high yields over very short periods, such as doubling your money in 90 days.

2. A few marks take advantage of the offer. The con artist uses the money from the second investor to pay instant returns to the first investor, the money from the third investor to pay the second one, and so on. The con artist is "robbing Peter to pay Paul."

The Sting

3. Seeing the instant high yields being enjoyed by the first marks, many more marks rush to take advantage of the offer. Blinded by their greed and the potential for making a fast buck, the marks don't pay too much attention to the supposed mechanics of the scheme, which allow it to pay such fantastic dividends. Ponzi schemes are particularly easy to pull during bull markets, when investors readily believe that immense growth over short periods is possible.

4. The con artist continues to use new income to meet old debts, while at the same time skimming a healthy profit off the top for himself. He may also start to employ agents to rope in more marks and may even set up an

The Players
a. The Con Artist
(AKA the rope or catch,
usually a female)
b. The Accomplice
(the cap)
c. The Mark
(AKA the pigeon)

office to take in money and give the enterprise a patina of legitimacy, often attracting more marks.

5. If anyone starts asking awkward questions the con artist can usually dazzle them with his pitch and then buys them off with the promise of higher yields.

6. For the scheme to continue functioning, an exponentially increasing number of investors must be roped in. Eventually there are no more available investors and the scheme collapses. Ideally the con artist makes off with as much loot as possible before this.

Variations
The Peter-to-Paul scam forms the basic pattern of a whole raft of white collar frauds. A good example is the practice of lapping. This is where an employee of a company steals funds from work and then uses funds from another account to cover up the hole in the finances, at the same time creating a slightly bigger hole that must be covered up with still more funds, and so on, until he is caught.

Ivan the Terrible: The inside trader scandal

If Enron was the scandal that bookended the bullish '90s, the Boesky insider trading scandal signaled the end of the era of '80s excess.

Ivan Boesky is the son of a Detroit delicatessen chain owner who first came to prominence in Wall Street during the 1970s as an arbitrageur. Arbitrage is a form of high-stakes gambling for people with sterner nerve and deeper pockets than the average investor. When a company becomes the target of a hostile take-over bid its share price can fluctuate wildly and common-or-garden investors get skittish. The arbitrageur takes on their holdings, so that they get out at a decent price while he takes the risk – and reaps the potentially enormous rewards if the takeover works out and the price goes up.

Arbitrage was a relatively small game until the 1980s, when aggressive young players launched takeover bids on well-established companies that they felt were ripe for the plucking. If they could raise big enough loans they could buy up enough stock to take over the company, break it up and sell off the pieces, pay off the loans and keep the massive profits. There was a surge in takeover activity, and the arbitrage market became too crowded and competitive for Boesky's taste.

So he decided to improve the odds by cheating. He would receive inside information from the companies or from traders involved in deals and get in on the act before takeovers became public. Fat profits were available to everyone involved so there was no shortage of help. Boesky arranged his deals through complex partnership set-ups that gave him the lion's share of profits but passed on losses to investors. He was making hundreds of millions, but worked ever harder as he was addicted to

Name: Ivan Boesky
Nationality: American
Years as a con: around 4
Amount earned: $2B
Years in jail: 3

money-making. His infamous "greed is healthy" speech to the Berkeley School of Business in 1985 served as the model for the Oscar-winning turn by Michael Douglas in the movie *Wall Street.*

One of Boesky's sources was Dennis Levine, an investment banker who got five per cent of profit accrued from the inside information he gave out, netting him $12 million. But he was caught by Securities and Exchange Commission (SEC) and ratted out Boesky. Boesky in turn agreed to cooperate, shopping other Wall Street fraudsters, even wearing a wire once to help entrap junk bond king Michael Milken. Milken was eventually to pay a fine of $600 million, and still had a billion left over.

Although Boesky was sentenced to three years and paid $50 million in fines and $50 million in illegal profit repayments, he nonetheless pulled a number of moves on the authorities. The SEC allowed him to dump $1.32 billion worth of shares before his fine was announced, to avoid upsetting the market, meaning that he got out at the top of the market, avoiding the 1987 crash. He was allowed to pay his fine with shares that promptly dropped in value by more than half. And he even managed to get a tax deduction on the profit repayments.

ART FRAUD

The Players
a. The Con Artist (often part of a telemarketing firm)
b. The Accomplice (the Appraiser)
c. The Mark

Ever since the boom days of the 1980s, art has been seen as a valid investment by a much larger section of the population than the small community of artists, dealers, and collectors. This has opened profitable new markets for the ingenious con artist, to whom a spurious artwork is just bait, and no different to a bogus stock or share.

The Set-Up

1. The con artist gets hold of a list of people who have bought or expressed interest in art – for example, subscribers to a gallery newsletter. Alternatively, the con artist gets the mark to get in touch through direct mail marketing, with letters offering free prints in a contest.

2. The con artist calls up the mark and makes the pitch. On offer is a very special, very limited edition print of a rare work by a highly prized artist. Apart from being beautiful and highly collectable, it is also such a great investment that it is practically guaranteed to go up in value.

3. The mark is stressed or deadlined with hurry-up tactics – for instance, the offer is only available for a limited time; or, even better, the artist is on his deathbed, and when he dies his work will rocket in value – but of course that could be any moment, so buy now!

4. Certificates of authenticity and provenance may well be offered, but these will be worthless. An additional service may also be offered – the services of an "independent" art appraiser to value the artwork. The appraiser is a cap, who will first soak the mark for extra fees before declaring the bogus work genuine.

The Sting

5. The mark hands over his credit card details and, in return, receives either nothing or a shoddy print worth a fraction of the reported value, which has no investment value whatsoever.

6. Any money-back guarantees will be revealed to be worthless or invalidated by small print (for example, the mark has the right to return his print in return for another one).

Variations

The con artist can be a genuine gallery owner or art dealer, and the bogus art on offer may be displayed along with genuine works of art. Favorite artists to fake include Salvador Dali, Pablo Picasso, Marc Chagall, and Joan Miro – anyone with high recognition value. One gallery-based scam is artwork reselling. The investor is encouraged to buy a piece as an investment on the basis that it will remain in the gallery to be displayed to other customers. The investor will recoup his investment plus interest when it is sold. This pitch is then repeated ad infinitum, so that many people end up "owning" the same artwork.

ATM SCAMS

The automated teller machine has proved a godsend to resourceful crooks and con artists, providing a range of scams to pull and removing the necessity to foil suspicious bank tellers or have to deal with a human being at all.

ATM Bombing
1. The con artist opens an account under a false name.
2. He then pays a check into his account via an envelope fed into an automated teller machine – he keys in the supposed amount (for example, $1,000) himself. A thousand dollars is instantly credited to the con artist's account.
3. The con artist uses his card to withdraw the maximum allowable amount from as many machines as possible, until he has used up all $1,000 of credit.
4. When the ATM's contents are checked the next day, the "check" that he deposited proves to be nothing more than a slip of blank paper.

ATM Tampering
1. The con artist fixes an official-looking notice to the ATM, informing unsuspecting customers that the minimum withdrawal from this machine is $300.
2. He uses superglue to seal shut the jaws of the cash delivery slot.
3. The hapless mark attempts to withdraw $300. When it doesn't emerge he goes into the bank to complain.
4. The con artist uses a crowbar to prize open the jaws of the cash delivery slot and makes off with loot.

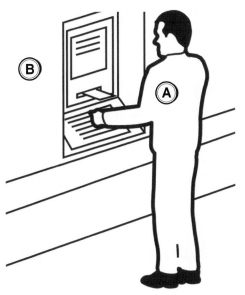

The Players

a. The Con Artist
b. The Mark
(the bank or bank customer)

ATM Faking

1. The con artist selects a stand-alone ATM in an isolated, infrequently checked area, and fits a false front onto it. The false front may have a slot for the card, a keyboard, and screen.

2. The unsuspecting mark tries to use the ATM, feeds in his card and uses the keypad to type in his PIN code.

3. The false front either swallows the card and displays an "out of order" message on the screen, or it uses a card reader or "skimmer" to scan and copy the magnetic strip on the card. Often the criminals will be sitting in a nearby car receiving the information transmitted to them from the scanner. This type of scam happens mostly at evenings and weekends, when the bank is closed.

4. The con artist either uses the card or a clone of the card, together with the PIN, which the false ATM has recorded, to withdraw cash from the mark's account.

5. Some ATM con artists even fit a tiny camera hidden in a harmless leaflet holder or other device which is mounted on the ATM in a position to be able to view and record customers' PIN numbers.

THE BOILER ROOM

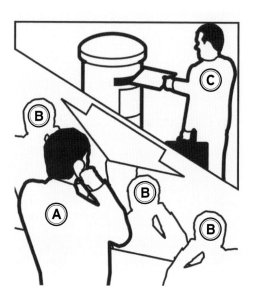

The Players

a. The Con Artist
(the bogus trader)

b. The Mark

Originally known as the Bucket Shop, the Boiler Room has achieved notoriety since the 1990s with telemarketing set-ups operating not just in America but also out of Thailand and states with poor security.

The Set-Up

1. The con artist, or his firm, get hold of a list of potential marks – people who might be interested in buying stocks or shares. Often marks are tagged when they respond to a direct mail shot or ask for more information about an investment opportunity that was advertised.

2. The con artist calls the mark and uses hard-sell tactics to pressure him into buying junk shares in a worthless company. Alternatively, the mark is offered an IPO – initial public offering. This is stock in a company that is only just floating on the stock market – its fortunes may depend on securing approval for a drug or product. Investing in an IPO is thus a gamble, but the con artist makes it sound like a sure thing, and may even claim to have inside knowledge. The stock is guaranteed to rise and if the mark is in from the start he could make a killing.

3. The Boiler Room (so-called because of its pressure-cooker atmosphere) uses various ruses to seem legitimate. It may be registered with an address on or near Wall Street, despite the fact that the con artist is actually calling from Thailand. Other con artists in the actual "boiler room" are encouraged to make noise so that it sounds like a real and highly successful trading floor.

4. The mark is deadlined to get him to agree to the deal quickly.

The Sting

5. The mark pays up and receives in return professional-looking, but practically worthless, stocks and shares. The boiler room makes its money from brokerage fees, by selling shares for more than they are worth, by getting kickbacks from the company they are pushing, or by selling entirely bogus shares and pocketing all of the money.

6. When the mark's shares inevitably fall in value he can still be gulled further. The con artist may call and reassure him that this only a temporary dip that offers a great opportunity to average down the price of his holding – if he buys more shares at this lower price, the average price for his total holding will be lower.

Variations

In the original Rag scam, the "bucket shop" or fake brokerage, was a big store front like the phony betting parlor used in the Wire (see page 114). Staff and other customers were all in on the scam, and the boards showed information about fake companies. The mark would be allowed to make an initial profit, based on "inside information" supplied by the con artist, and then taken for a large investment.

Charles Ponzi: Robbing Peter to pay Paul

Name: Charles Ponzi
Nationality: Italian
Years as a con: 31
Amount earned: $10 to 20M
Years in jail: 17

Today the Ponzi Scheme is one of the best known forms of investment fraud, closely related to the even more infamous Pyramid Scheme. Although Ponzi was not the first to practice this con, his version was the biggest and best.

Born in Italy in 1882, Charles Ponzi came to America in 1903. He got a job in a restaurant but was fired for short-changing the customers. He moved to Montreal and got a job in a bank, but ran into trouble with the law for forging checks and did three years in a Canadian prison. He told his mother that he'd got a job as an assistant to the warden. On his release he moved back to the States but once more landed in jail, this time for involvement in an illegal immigration scam. Finally, in 1918, he came to Boston where he got a job and married a nice Italian girl. Soon after he hit upon a brilliant – and legal – scheme to make money. At the time it was common for Italian immigrants writing back to the Old Country to send a postal reply coupon with their letter.

The recipient could use the coupon to pay the return postage when replying. The key was that coupons were four times cheaper in Italy than in the US. By engaging in what was essentially a form of currency trading, Ponzi realized that he could take advantage of this discrepancy to make a 400 percent profit. He would send money to Italy where a friend would buy up coupons and send them back for resale in the US. It was all perfectly legal and it worked.

Word spread and soon investors were beating a path to Ponzi's door. He set up the Securities Exchange Company and employed agents to bring in more cash. Money started to flood in.

Up until this point, Ponzi's scam was not a Ponzi Scheme – he was able to pay off the first few investors with genuine profits. But almost immediately the flaw in his plan surfaced – international reply coupons were small value items of which few were in circulation. The market for trading in them on a large scale simply didn't exist. To make good his new investments Ponzi started down the road to his doom – he began to "rob Peter to pay Paul" in classic Ponzi-scheme fashion (see page 130).

By May 1920 Ponzi had taken in $420,000. By July he was taking in a quarter of a million dollars a day! He became a hero to the local immigrant community and people began investing their life savings with him. Inevitably the house of cards came crashing down. An investigation by the *Boston Post* revealed the basic flaw in the Ponzi scheme – to cover all the investments there would have to be 160 million international reply coupons in circulation, but in reality there were fewer than 30,000. In August, 1920, Ponzi was indicted on 86 counts of fraud, and despite outrage among his supporters he was jailed. Eventually he was deported. He never became a US citizen and he died in poverty in Brazil, in 1948.

Scams for the Information Age

The advent of the Internet has opened up new vistas of opportunity for the con artist – new media through which to conduct old scams, and new types of scam altogether. It has been likened to the Wild West – a lawless frontier impossible to police, where the hustler and grifter have free rein. Certainly the very nature of the Internet makes it hard to police, contain, or control. Shut off one server, node, or ISP and the criminals can simply move to another. Make something illegal in one country and the criminals simply operate out of a different one.

The Information Age also increases the confidence artist's opportunity to get hold of a person's personal and financial information. It is increasingly routine to send credit card and bank details across the Internet for on-line shopping and services, and the vast majority of people have no concept of how computer security and information transfer work. E-mail in particular has been a godsend to the con artist. The con artist now has a fool-proof way of getting in touch with a vast number of people at zero cost to himself with no way of being traced and no need to make physical contact. The con artist can pretend to be anyone, anywhere, and frequently does . . .

Another, entirely new arena of scamming opportunity is the on-line auction. According to the Internet Fraud Complaint Center, on-line auction fraud (which basically means either not delivering items or delivering ones inferior to those advertised) is the most common form of Internet scam, accounting for over 60 percent of complaints.

IDENTITY THEFT

The Players
a. The Con Artist
b. The Mark

According to the US Justice Department, up to 700,000 people have their identity stolen each year in America alone, with con artists using their personal details to steal money and cover their tracks. People whose identities have been stolen can spend years trying to retrieve their good name and their credit record. Victims may lose job opportunities, be refused loans, housing or cars, or could even get arrested for crimes they didn't commit.

The Set-Up
1. The con artist picks his mark, either through opportunity (perhaps buying a list of credit card numbers on the Internet) or by targeting them specifically (for example, using the *Forbes* "Rich List" to pick wealthy marks). He gathers as much information about the mark as possible and starts with the phone book to get the mark's address.

2. The con artist locates the address and goes through the mark's trash to find old bank statements, credit card statements, bills, letters from insurance companies or government agencies and junk mail offers of pre-approved credit cards and loans.

3. The con artist then visits the Public Records Office to discover dates of birth, marriage, etc, and to order a copy of the mark's birth certificate.

4. By calling up one of the credit reporting companies and posing as a landlord who is running a credit check on a prospective tenant, the con artist obtains the mark's complete credit history.

5. The con artist goes on-line to buy other relevant information from other criminals – in particular details about the mark such as his Social Security number.

The Sting

6. Using his illicitly gleaned information, the con artist applies for credit cards, opens bank accounts and takes out loans, all in the mark's name.

7. He spends as much money as possible, as quickly as possible, maxing out all the credit cards, spending the loans, and writing rubber checks to purchase high value goods, which he can then pawn or sell on, pocketing the cash.

8. The mark doesn't realize what's going on at first because the con artist has used the stolen ID info with a fake address, or even had redirect placed on the mail sent the mark's home address. He has also had the mark's phone number delisted to prevent the mark hearing from creditors. When all the credit is exhausted, the con artist moves on to steal another identity leaving the banks and credit card companies chasing the mark for payment.

9. Depending on how far the con artist is willing to go, he uses the fake ID details to get a driver's license or even a passport, and carries out a variety of crimes and cons under his assumed identity. The police end up looking for the wrong guy.

HALL OF FAME

The Baron of Arizona:
The great Arizona land grab

Name: James Addison Reavis
Nationality: American
Years as a con: around 30
Amount earned: $Millions
Years in jail: 2

The tale of James Reavis, sometime St Louis real estate agent and erstwhile Baron de Peralta, owner of Arizona and intimate of the royal families of Spain and Britain, offers a unique glimpse of frontier days gone by and the power politics of late-nineteenth-century American expansion.

Reavis's story begins in 1843, when he was born to an itinerant laborer and a half-Spanish mother in the Missouri Territory. During the Civil War, Reavis discovered a talent for forgery, making bogus passes for himself and anyone who could pay. By 1869 he had set up shop in St Louis as a mostly legitimate realtor, only occasionally resorting to his forgery skills to help with tricky documents.

In 1871 he met a colorful frontier character named Dr George Willing, who claimed to possess a document granting him possession of thousands of square miles of Arizona territory, way out west. Supposedly Willing had bought the grant from a line of impoverished Spanish noblemen, the Peraltas. Although the story sounded bogus, Reavis wondered if there was something to the old man's tale. In 1874 Willing died, so Reavis decamped to Arizona and finally saw the Peralta land grant documents. Reavis realized that he needed to employ his forgery skills to improve the provenance of the claim. He visited record offices in Mexico, pored over grants, deeds, and maps, and hatched a plan of far greater scope. He forged a ream of documents, inventing a bogus Peralta lineage and establishing a claim to practically the whole of Arizona.

He returned to Arizona in 1882 and, using the mass of forgeries as back up, claimed that he was no less than the Baron of Arizonac [sic], and that every landowner and tenant in Arizona owed him rent. He employed an army of lawyers and thugs to go round the country extorting money, and succeeded in attracting millions in investment for development schemes by issuing bogus shares in inflated companies.

He married a poor but beautiful Spanish-American girl and trained her to become a grand lady, inventing a complex lineage that made her sole heir to the great Peralta dynasty. Reavis became Baron Peralta. With the help of powerful friends, Reavis secured introductions to the most powerful people in Spain and the pair became the toast of Spanish society, courted by financiers eager to regain a foothold in the new American territories. In 1887 the couple visited Britain and took part in the Golden Jubilee celebrations as guests of Queen Victoria.

Returning to Arizona, Reavis sued the government for refusing to acknowledge his claim to Arizona. But an investigation demolished every aspect of his claim, revealing the trail of forgeries. When the case came to court in 1895 he was arrested and found guilty of fraud and forgery. He emerged in 1898 to live out the rest of his days a bitter man, poring over documents in the library. He died in 1914.

THE NIGERIAN E-MAIL "419" SCAM

Known by the section of Nigerian law that deals with fraud (419), the now notorious Nigerian e-mail scam fleeces people of millions of dollars a year, and, in some cases, may even have culminated in murder.

The Set-Up

1. The con artist goes to a cyber-café in Lagos, Nigeria, and opens a hotmail account under a fake name.

2. He writes an e-mail setting out his pitch, in which he claims to be a high-ranking member of Nigerian society or government. He claims to have access to a huge sum of money which must be moved out of Nigeria, preferably via the mark's bank account, in return for which the mark will receive an impressive commission. Usually the money is dirty in some way, for example, resulting from over-invoicing of government contracts – so the whole thing must be kept discreet.

3. If possible the con artist gets a list of e-mail addresses and picks out people who are professionals or businesspeople, in which case the e-mail begins by explaining that the mark is being offered this opportunity as "a trustworthy and honorable person whose name has been recommended to me." If not, he simply mass-mails to "Dear Sir/Madam."

The Sting

4. The mark cautiously replies that he would be happy to make millions for such a small service. The con artist replies with more juicy details about how much the mark will earn, but also reveals that in order to free

The Players

a. The Con Artist
b. The Accomplices (police impersonators)
c. The Mark

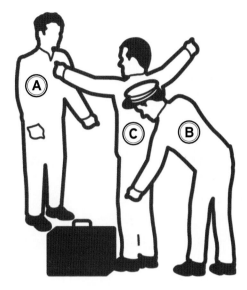

up the money from the accounts where it is held, it will be necessary to advance money to cover expenses, such as banking fees, service charges, or bribes, for example.

5. The con artist continues to invent new expenses while also keeping the mark informed of the progress of the deal. The more money the mark has invested in the scheme, the more he wants to believe that it will pay off and the more likely he is to continue coughing up.

6. Particularly ambitious con artists may even invite the mark to Nigeria to check up on progress and smooth the path of the deal. When the mark arrives he is immediately picked up by accomplices posing as police and shaken down for more money. According to some reports, marks with a beef have wound up dead.

Variations

The "419" scam has also been perpetrated via fax and letter for many years, but with the move to the on-line medium its reported incidence went up by 900 percent in just one year, according to US consumer lobby the National Consumers League.

SKIMMING: CREDIT CARD CLONING

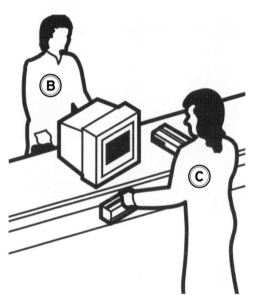

The Players
a. The Con Artist
b. The Mark
c. The Accomplice (the outside man, cap or gopher)

Skimming, the copying of credit card details by swiping the card through a special reader, is a fast-growing crime estimated to cost credit card issuers more than $350,000 a day – over £420 million ($600 million) in the UK alone in 2002. The scam takes place all over the world and is mainly run by organized gangs based in Russia and Eastern Europe. The majority of "skims" take place in London, England, but can take place anywhere, so it pays to be aware.

The Set-Up

1. The con artist approaches waiters, shop assistants or barmen to act as the front man or gopher, for the operation. Often people from the same ethnic background as the con artist will be recruited.

2. The gopher is given a small electronic device known as a "skimmer."

The Sting

3. When a customer pays his bill with a credit card (gold or platinum cards are preferred because they carry a higher credit limit), the gopher takes the card behind the counter, round the corner or similarly out of sight. He then swipes the card once through the legitimate card reader as usual, and then again through the skimmer. The skimmer scans the card and stores the information recorded on the card's magnetic strip.

4. After storing the details of up to 150 cards on the skimmer, the gopher sells it back to the con artist for around $150. The details are then downloaded from the skimmer onto a computer. Depending on the level of technology available, the con artist either uses the credit card details to make "card not present" purchases, such as over the Internet (according to the European Commission, purchases from on-line shopping sites contributed to a 50 percent rise in card fraud in Europe during 2000), or clones the card by copying the details on to the magnetic strip of another card. This may be someone else's stolen card, a non-credit card or a specially made credit card that mimics the mark's card. The con artist can use an embossing machine and even fix on holographic transfers. All this takes less than a day.

5. The cloned card is either sold on to other criminals (usually for between $400 and $600) or used by the con artist himself. High-value or easily resold goods are purchased over the next two or three days before the cloned card is discarded. Favorite goods to buy are laptop computers and CDs. The mark doesn't realize he's been had until his statement arrives at the end of the month.

6. Advice for avoiding credit card skims is to be suspicious if a retail employee swipes you card through two devices instead of one – the second device could be a skimmer. Always take your credit card slips with you, as a crook could find useful information printed on them.

PHISHING

The Players
a. The Con Artist (AKA the programmer)
b. The Mark

Since 1996, computer-literate criminals have been taking advantage of public familiarity with Internet credit card transactions with a con known as e-mail culling or "phishing," from the hacker spelling of "fishing."

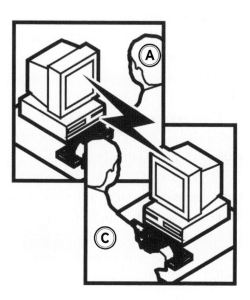

The Set-Up
1. The con artist sets up a fake website that looks exactly the same as the website of a reputable financial Internet company, such as Amazon, or a transaction-handling company such as PayPal. The fake site will resemble the web-page of the real company that deals with account management, with spaces for the mark to type in credit card numbers and passwords.
2. The con artist registers the fake web-page with a URL address very similar to the mimicked company. For instance, one phishing con based on PayPal used the URL www.PcyPal.com.
3. The con artist e-mails thousands of potential marks purporting to be from the fake company, warning that there is a problem with his account

and he needs to confirm his details. Included in the e-mail is a hyperlink that the mark can click on to go straight there. The mark thinks he's clicking on a link to PayPal but is actually he is being taken somewhere quite different.

The Sting

4. When the mark clicks on the bogus hyperlink he is taken to the bogus web-page and, dutifully and unsuspectingly, fills in his details where requested, including name, account number, address, and card details.
5. The bogus web-page feeds this info to the con artist, who uses it to make extensive purchases or raid the mark's bank account. It could even be used for identity theft.

WATCHING THE DETECTIVES

ANTI-CARD FRAUD

As we come to rely ever more on plastic, so card scams are becoming more prevalent. With little law enforcement in this area, card companies are taking matters into their own hands. Private anti-fraud groups are now employed to track down the fraud gangs, and new technology is helping to protect cards and make cloning impossible. "Smart" cards with built-in computer chips storing cardholder's details in encrypted form are already widely used, but the biggest advance is the introduction of PIN numbers, which must be typed by hand into small terminals at the point of payment. This system has cut card fraud by 50 percent in France.

Vladimir Levin: The first cyberheist

Name: Vladimir Levin
Nationality: Russian
Years as a con: 1
Amount earned: $10M
Years in jail: 3

Levin was the central figure in a 1994 cybercrime that changed the way the banking world thinks about computer fraud and cyber-protection.

The Citibank cyber-raid began in August, 1994, when the head trader at Argentina's Invest Capital, noticed that his company's cash management account had been drained of $200,000 overnight. The company's bankers, Citibank, were alerted and they quickly realized that this was not an isolated incident. Other accounts around the globe were being raided, the money siphoned off to nameless accounts in California, Latin America, Finland, Israel, and the Netherlands. Eventually more than 20 accounts were hit for a total of $10 million.

The FBI were called in and they traced some of the stolen money to an account in San Francisco. Lying in wait, they pounced on a Russian woman, Ekaterina Korolkov, who was attempting to withdraw the dodgy dollars. She confessed that the money had, indeed, come from Citibank, and pointed the finger at her husband, Evgueni. He too cut a deal with the authorities, spilling the beans. It seemed the cyber-swindle was the work of the Russian mafia, who were using a mild-mannered, ex-academic named Vladimir Levin to mastermind the scam. Somehow Citibank and the FBI had to trace the illicit transfer to him and get the decisive evidence. Unfortunately, the antiquated telephone system of the old Soviet bloc made this difficult, leaving no record of calls made or received. In other words, they would have to catch Levin in the act.

Citibank agreed to another illegal money transfer. US Military Intelligence traced it to Rotterdam, the Netherlands, where the police picked up another Russian, Vladimir Veronin, attempting to withdraw $1 million. Veronin again pointed the finger at Levin, who, he said, worked from a down-at-heel IT outfit in St Petersburg.

A raid on the AO Saturn offices revealed computers, guns, and Levin's passport but no hard evidence, but in 1995 Levin was picked up at London's Stansted Airport and extradited to the US. Under questioning, a strange story emerged. Levin, a biotechnology graduate, sour at the low wages he received, was recruited by the Russian mafia to hack Citibank systems using a system developed by a secretive Russian intellectual known only as Megazoid. Megazoid claims to have been the first to hack Citibank's systems but insists he has no interest in stealing money. He keeps his identity secret to avoid being co-opted by the mafia.

Using Megazoid's system, Levin was able to tap into Citibank's transactions and steal clients' PIN numbers and account details. From a simple laptop he was then able to access their accounts and shift money around the globe. Citibank claims that it recovered all but $400,000 of the stolen money, and now has the world's most advanced computer protection system. Levin got three years and a hefty fine.

GLOSSARY

Ace, having the: Having arrangements with local authorities to protect a scamming activity.
Advance man: An accomplice who scouts the locale and the mark.
Angle: The approach or role taken by the con artist.
Apple: A mark.
Badge-play comeback: A follow-up scam where the con artist poses as a law-enforcement agent and approaches previously duped marks pretending to help, but in reality scamming them out of more money.
Badger game: Any confidence trick where sex is used as bait for the mark.
Bait-and-switch: Any con trick where the mark is promised one thing and left with another.
Bankroll: To fund a scamming operation.
Bates: A mark.
Beef: To complain about being scammed, either to the con artist or the authorities.
Big store: A con game involving a fake establishment that the mark believes to be real.
Bilk: To con, scam, grift, or hustle.
Block/block hustle: A ruse or device to prevent the mark from beefing. Also a specific con involving pretending to sell stolen merchandise.
Blow-off: Where a con game is wound up and the con artist makes his getaway.
Boiler room: A bucket shop; in modern parlance a bucket shop for aggressive telemarketing.
Broads: The cards used in the Three-card Monte con game.
Broad-tosser: A card sharp practicing the Three-card Monte con game.
Bucket shop: A fake brokerage used in a Big Store con.
Bunco/bunko: A con or the act of conning.
Bunco squad: Department at local police level that specializes in cons and scams.
Button: A fake police raid staged to effect a block.
Cackle-bladder: A squib of fake blood.
Cap/capper: An accomplice of a con artist; similar to a shill.
Catch: *see* Roper.
Card sharp: Someone who is skilled at dealing, shuffling, and, usually, cheating at cards.
Check-hanging: *see* Paper-kiting.
Cold reading: The tactics used by fake psychics, mind readers, and other con artists to glean information from a person, mainly through conversation, without their knowledge.
Contact man: Someone who is, or pretends to be, the person one is supposed to contact on arrival somewhere.
Convincer: A ruse or device that increases the mark's enthusiasm for the con trick by allowing him to temporarily profit.
Country send: A send practiced on a rube.
Deadlining: A ruse or device used to pressure the mark into acting fast.
Depot worker: A con artist who works transport hubs, such as stations and airports.

Dupe: A mark or the act of deceiving someone.

Faro: A complicated card game beloved of nineteenth-century gamblers and con men.

Fix: Having arrangements with the local authorities to protect scamming activity.

Fraud, actual: A crime involving lying about the existence of promised goods or services.

Fraud, constructive: A crime involving misleading statements or actions about promised goods or services.

Fraud, wire: A legal term, describing fraud committed using the telephone or Internet.

Green: Inexperienced or naïve mark.

Gopher: In a skimming con, the accomplice who actually skims the credit cards.

Grift: A con or the act of conning.

Grifter: A con artist; usually implies a low class con artist – one who works short cons.

Gull: A mark or the act of deceiving someone.

Heat: The law, or the attentions of the law.

Heavy: *see* Muscle.

Hot reading: A false psychic reading based on information previously gleaned about the mark through research or spying.

Hot seat: A ruse in a rigged card game where the mark appears to have unbeatable hand.

Hurrah: That part of a con trick where the mark is drawn into such an extent that he is fully committed to seeing the con through.

Hustler: A con artist; usually implies even lower class con artist than a grifter.

Inside man: The main con artist in a long con.

Insider: A person working within an organization who is "in on the scam."

John: A mark.

Kickback: An illegal payment offered in return for directing funds toward someone.

Lapping: Where an employee steals funds from work and then uses funds from another account to cover up the hole in the finances, and so on.

Lemon: A rigged card game where con artists work together to cheat the mark.

Long con: A con trick where the con artist meets with the mark more than once.

Lost-and-found wallet: *see* Magic wallet.

Lugger: *see* Roper.

Magic wallet: A prop used to convince the mark of a con artist's wealth and importance.

Managed earnings scam: An investment fraud where a company lies about its earnings and "manages" its books to maintain the share price and attract investors.

Mich roll: Short for Michigan roll; a wad of blank paper or small-denomination bills wrapped in a few high-denomination bills.

Middleman: An accomplice who acts as roper or steerer in long cons.

Moxy: Guts, front, nerve, chutzpah.

Mr Goodman: A mark.

Muscle: A threatening or large accomplice who provides physical strength.

Palm: To surreptitiously pick up or conceal an item in the hand, without anyone noticing.

Panel game: A type of badger game where a con artist slips into a room via a secret panel to relieve the sleeping mark of his valuables.

Panhandling: Asking for money from strangers; begging.

Paper-kiting: The act of passing forged checks.

Peter-to-Paul: A scam that involves stealing more money to cover previous debts.

Phishing: Sending bogus e-mails to elicit personal details from the mark.

Pigeon drop: A scam based on money "found" in the street.

Pitch: Where the con artist seeks to gain the interest and/or participation of the mark.

Point-out: The part of a con game where the inside man is pointed out to the mark as someone of influence and power.

Ponzi scheme: An investment fraud; a generic name for Peter-to-Paul type scams.

Props: Items used to help stage a con.

Pseudoscience: A topic that poses as genuine science by using the trappings of science, but which has not been properly tested or proven.

Putting on the dog: Assuming the appearance and habits of a rich person as part of a con.

Pyramid scheme: A financial scam based on recruiting marks to recruit other marks.

Rag: A " bucket shop."

Red-inking: A threat to cut the mark out of a deal; made to frighten him into compliance.

Rig: The fake establishment used in a Big Store con.

Rigged: Previously set-up or arranged to allow cheating.

Ringer: Something worthless that can be swapped for something of value.

Roper: An accomplice who "ropes" in marks.

Rube: A simple type from the country.

Ruse: A trick; a strategem to deceive, cheat or misdirect.

Send: The part of a con trick where the mark is sent home or to the bank to get his money.

Set-up: The part of a con trick where the trick is arranged and set in motion.

Shell game: A version of Three-card monte involving a ball and three cups or shells.

Shill: An accomplice who lures the mark often by pretending to be a member of the public.

Short con: Any scam where the con artist comes into contact with the mark only once.

Skimming: Copying a credit card's details by swiping it through a special reader.

Sociopath: Someone who lacks conscience, morality, empathy, etc.

Spanish handkerchief: A con game where a switch is effected using a handkerchief or bag.

Stall: Temporarily preventing the mark from getting involved, to increase his motivation.

Steerer: *see* Roper.

Sting: The part of a con trick where the aim of the trick is achieved.

Stress: The part of a con trick where the mark is deadlined or pressured into action.

Sweetheart scam: Any confidence game based around a bogus romantic relationship between the mark and the con artist.

Switch: Where money or other valuables are switched for something worthless.

Tap: To obtain money from someone.

Tear-up: The part of a con trick where the con artist appears to release the mark from his obligations so that he leaves without argument – typically pretending to tear-up a check.

Three-card monte: A gambling short con involving trying to guess which of three shuffled cards is the red queen.

Whistleblower: An insider who exposes shady or illegal practice by an organization.

Wire: A phony bookies used in a Big Store con.

INDEX